Why, as a Muslim, I Defend Liberty

Mustafa Akyol

CATO INSTITUTE
WASHINGTON, DC

Copyright © 2021 Cato Institute.
All rights reserved.

Print ISBN: 978-1-952223-17-4
eBook ISBN: 978-1-952223-18-1

Library of Congress Cataloging-in-Publication Data available.
Library of Congress Control Number: 2021939010

Cover design: Molly von Borstel, Faceout Studio

Printed in Canada.

CATO INSTITUTE
1000 Massachusetts Avenue NW
Washington, DC 20001
www.cato.org

Dedicated to my lovely little sons,
Levent Taha, Efe Rauf, and Danin Murad

Without liberty . . . humans are degraded into instruments.
[So] liberty is the witness of human dignity;
if there is no liberty, there will be no dignity.
Liberty is also the source of all kinds of progress;
if there is no liberty, there will no progress.

—Münif Pasha, Ottoman statesman and intellectual,
1830-1910

CONTENTS

Introduction: Why Liberty Matters

> To compel individuals to confess a faith . . . creates not a religious society, but a monolithic and terrified mass of crippled, submissive, and hypocritical subjects.
>
> —Abdolkarim Soroush, Iranian Islamic philosopher[1]

In January 2013, when I was still living in my hometown, Istanbul, I flew to Riyadh, the Saudi capital, to attend a conference on the politics of the Middle East. The event was interesting, my Saudi hosts were gracious, and it was an experience to visit the kingdom for the second time after an *umra* (little pilgrimage) to Mecca two years before. But I had the most interesting experience on the Turkish Airlines plane that took me home.

In Riyadh, all women boarded the plane fully covered. To be more specific, all of them wore plain black dresses that covered them from head to toe, showing, at most, only their faces. About half of the women were covered up even more: they were wearing the *niqab* (face veil), which showed only their eyes. When the plane approached Istanbul, however, I noticed some of these women walk back to the lavatory and emerge dressed in a very different fashion. Now, they were all wearing much more relaxed dresses—a few of which were quite revealing—along with heavy makeup. One woman, I can say, was wearing one of the shortest miniskirts I had ever seen. Apparently, she was ready to party in Istanbul's famous nightclubs.

When I viewed this scene, I did not judge those women. One could have blamed them for hypocrisy, but that would be unfair. They were not *choosing* hypocrisy—wearing ultraconservative dresses within Saudi Arabia, and something quite different when they stepped outside. Rather, it was imposed on them. The Kingdom of Saudi Arabia—with its rigid religious laws and its notorious religion police—was forcing them to do something they did not want to do.

Moreover, this problem was not limited to Saudi Arabia. The Islamic Republic of Iran—a bitter rival but also a like-minded counterpart—also dictates that all women wear the headscarf, despite resistance and defiance among them. Similar dictates, either by law or by custom, have also taken place in certain countries of the Arab world, Afghanistan, Pakistan, Malaysia, and Indonesia.

This, of course, does not mean that *all* women in those countries cover themselves unwillingly. No, not at all. Worldwide, many Muslim women believe that a conservative dress and a head cover are requirements of their religion, which they willingly observe. To assume that they all must be doing this because of the dictates of men—or some "false consciousness" instilled in them by men—has led to contradictory dictates. French authorities, most notably, have banned the Islamic headscarf in public schools and jobs, as well as the "burkini"—a swimsuit that covers the body and the hair—on some of their beaches. Similar bans have been issued in Belgium; Quebec, Canada; and even Turkey, which used to adopt an illiberal version of secularism until the early 2010s.

What Does Liberty Mean?

In all the cases mentioned—more severely in Saudi Arabia and Iran, where dictates are much more sweeping and stricter—what we see is the lack of a value that is crucial for human dignity, happiness, and flourishing: liberty. It is the value I will discuss in this book, in its relation to Islam.

What does "liberty" mean exactly? The *New Oxford American Dictionary* defines it as "the state of being free within society from oppressive restrictions imposed by authority on one's way of life, behavior, or political views." More briefly, liberty is also defined as "the absence of coercive constraint."[2] Such constraints on the individual may come from the government, society, or other individuals. And because the relationship between these three realms—the state, society, and the individual—is a matter of politics, liberty is primarily a political concept.

It is important to make that point clear, because some people may suppress liberty by claiming that they are actually serving some "real liberty." For example, the Saudi religious police or Iranian Revolutionary Guards who impose dress codes on women may claim to bring these women "liberty from immorality" or "liberty from Western cultural imperialism."

Conversely, an atheist dictatorship may close down all churches and mosques by claiming to bring "liberty from superstition"—which is exactly what happened in Albania during the communist regime of Enver Hoxha (1941–1985). That regime vowed to "liberate people from religious beliefs and backward customs."[3] As I was writing those lines, another communist dictatorship, China, was also claiming to "liberate" its Uyghur Muslim minority, by enslaving millions among them in "reeducation" camps. It was also proudly "emancipating" Uyghur women from "being baby-making machines"—in a genocidal campaign of forced abortion and sterilization.[4]

In other words, there may be regimes, groups, or individuals in the world who attack our liberty in order to serve some higher good that they themselves have chosen for us. We, obviously, should not be misled by their pretense.

An important thinker who stressed this point was John Stuart Mill, a 19th-century British philosopher. In his landmark 1859 book, *On Liberty*, he wrote the following:

> The only purpose for which power can be rightfully exercised over any member of a civilized community, against his will, is to prevent harm to others. His own good, either physical or moral, is not a sufficient warrant.[5]

Mill was one of architects of the political philosophy called "liberalism," which was born in early modern Europe with an emphasis on individual liberty, consent of the governed, and equality before the law. Some of its advocates—including Mill—had Eurocentric biases and double standards, which was then common, but liberalism matured over time, championing *universal* human rights, for everyone, everywhere. It was also adopted by many non-Westerners, including

Muslims, who promoted liberal values in their societies, for the sake of those societies—an important point to which I will return later in this book.

Variants and nuances of liberalism, and their implications in real life, are endlessly discussed by political theorists and public intellectuals. Also, the term has taken slightly different meanings in different contexts—implying often "classical liberalism" in Europe, which is what I am talking about here, while implying a center-left progressivism in America, where the term "libertarianism" emerged as a helpful clarification. And even those who define themselves as "liberal" or "libertarian" may disagree on how these ideas must be applied to specific cases.

All those nuances and complications of liberalism, however, are not my focus in this book. My focus is whether its core value—liberty, in the sense of "the absence of coercive constraint"—is compatible with Islam.

The Argument in a Nutshell

In a nutshell, here is my argument:

- First, liberty *is* compatible with Islam—if it is understood as a voluntary faith, and not a coercive system. That is because Islam, at its core, rests on the sincere relationship between God and the individual, which can exist only in a medium of freedom, not coercion. The latter, as I observed on my Riyadh–Istanbul flight, can create only hypocrisy, not piety.

- However, quite a few Muslims understand Islam, indeed, as a coercive system—a system that will dictate piety by force, while eradicating impiety, apostasy, or blasphemy, also by force. Moreover, those coercive Muslims are not groundless: they rely on traditional interpretations of the Sharia—Islamic law—which needs a frank discussion, and some major reinterpretation, for Islam to be compatible with liberty.

- Yet there is also better news: the two fundamental sources of the Sharia—the Qur'an and the Prophetic example—also include "seeds of freedom," as Catholic scholar Daniel Philpott calls them.[6] These seeds show that the values of modern-day liberalism also had Islamic roots, which require some excavation and cultivation today.

I will expand on these points in the chapters ahead. They are essays in themselves that may be read separately, but they are interwoven. Their aim is not to be exhaustive but to offer perspectives and insights. And here is how they will proceed.

First, in Chapter 1, I will show the first "seed of freedom" in the Qur'an, but also how it is circumvented by Muslims who believe in coercion. We will also see how similar the latter's worldview is to that of the coercive Christians challenged by John Locke, the father of liberalism, back in the 17th century.

In Chapters 2 and 3, we will first see the burning need to "rethink" the Sharia—by separating the human from the divine and also by realizing the "intentions" of the divine. Then, we will see what lesson and inspiration we can derive from the Sharia for a crucial liberal value that is painfully lacking in the modern Muslim world: rule of law.

In Chapters 4 and 5, we will use a thought experiment—an island-state established by shipwreck survivors—to reconsider the politics of Islam. Does Islam call for conquest and supremacy, as some Muslims believe? Or should Muslims cherish political systems based on contract and equality? Meanwhile, does Islam really oblige its believers to "obey" their rulers, leaders, or some other great men?

Chapter 6 will address a common concern among Muslims: How can we allow all those irreverent atheists and offensive blasphemers to talk freely against our religion? Should we not silence them?

Chapter 7 will go into the economics of liberalism and see why that much-derided term "capitalism" is not alien to Islam but rather intrinsic to it, even in its conservative interpretations.

Finally, in Chapter 8, I will get to a question that may haunt some Muslims the moment they hear the word "liberty," let alone "liberalism": Aren't these the ideas of the colonizers that have invaded and plundered Muslim lands in the past 200 years? Why would we buy into their narratives? Is this some neocolonial conspiracy?

Surely, all these questions require much longer discussions than what I could summarize in this little book. Some of them also call for a deeper engagement with Islamic theology and philosophy that I offer in my more comprehensive book, which I would strongly recommend: *Reopening Muslim Minds: A Return to Reason, Freedom, and Tolerance* (St. Martin's Press, 2021).

Yet this book does another job: elucidating complex ideas with personal anecdotes, historical episodes, and thought experiments, which I am sharing for the first time. It also addresses some topics I have not covered anywhere else.

Naturally, I don't know where you personally stand, dear reader, on either Islam or liberty. But no matter where you stand, all I hope is that you may join me in thinking about them.

1

Is There Some Compulsion in Islam?

Now the truth has come from your Lord: let those who wish to believe in it do so, and let those who wish to reject it do so.

— Qur'an, 18:29[7]

The right to choose is not between religion and irreligion. If [people] choose wrongly, they will be punished.

— Ali Qaderi, Iranian diplomat[8]

In Islam, what really is the status of liberty—in the sense of "absence of coercive constraint"?

The right place to begin searching for an answer is the most fundamental source of Islam—the Qur'an, which we Muslims believe to be the word of God revealed to the Prophet Muhammad, at different junctures in his 23-year-long Prophetic mission.

When you do that, and read the Qur'an from the beginning, you will probably not miss Verse 256 of the second *sura* (chapter). It reads as follows:

> *There is no compulsion in religion*: true guidance has become distinct from error, so whoever rejects false gods and believes in God has grasped the firmest hand-hold, one that will never break. God is all hearing and all knowing.[9]

The very first clause of this verse—"There is no compulsion in religion"—is quite a remarkable statement, especially when we recall that it was revealed at a time—the early 7th century—when the notion of "religious freedom" was not yet fashionable anywhere in the world, including the barren, harsh, and tribal Arabian Peninsula.

Things get even more remarkable when we look into what the verse may have meant in its original context. We are helped here by the Islamic literature on *asbab-al nuzul* (occasions of revelation), which informs us about the background of at least some of the Qur'anic verses. Regarding the verse in question, 2:256, the earliest "occasion" chronicler, al-Wahidi (d. 1075), reports two different narrations, both of which are placed in Medina—that is when early Muslims had the political power to exert compulsion, if they chose to. According to the first narration, the verse was revealed to the Prophet when some Arab women wanted to convert their children, who had grown up among the city's Jews and naturally adopted Judaism, to Islam. According to the second narration, the verse was revealed when a Muslim man, who had sons who adopted Christianity before the emergence of Islam, wanted to convert those sons again to Islam.[10]

According to both narrations, in other words, the Qur'anic Verse 2:256 ruled out forced conversions into Islam. And that, we must note, is a remarkable point. Because while it is usual for religions to oppose compulsion when it works *against* them, it is less usual for them to oppose compulsion when it works *for* them.

It is also notable that this Qur'anic "seed of freedom" allowed securing some level of religious freedom for non-Muslims in the premodern Islamic world. Admittedly, Muslims conquered lands, imposed Islamic rule, and treated non-Muslims only as second-class citizens—a triumphalist legacy I will later question in Chapter 4. That "hierarchical tolerance" was quite short of full citizenship with equal rights found in the modern world, but it was still preferable to the common alternative in the premodern world: forced conversion.[11] That is why many Sephardic Jews—who had to choose between Catholicism or persecution in 15th-century Spain—fled to Muslim lands, especially the Ottoman Empire, where they found the freedom to live, worship, and even flourish as Jews.[12] Many Eastern Christians, too, some of them Arabs, preserved their faiths for centuries under Islamic rule.[13]

However, the same premodern Islamic world also dramatically minimized the scope of the freedom implied by the Qur'anic clause "There is no compulsion in religion." This was once noted by Sheikh Abdur Rehman, a former chief justice of Pakistan, who praised the verse as "a charter of freedom of conscience unparalleled in the religious annals of mankind." Yet "with regret," he added, "one notices attempts made by Muslim scholars themselves to whittle down its broad humanistic meaning."[14]

The scholars in question—those who developed the Sharia (Islamic law), through jurisprudence—did this "whittling down" by establishing two grim categories of compulsion in religion. Although actual practices in Muslim societies could be often more lenient, in principle,

- "Apostasy," which is publicly abandoning Islam, was declared a crime punishable by death. In other words, while nobody was forced to enter Islam, once they entered it, even by birth, they would be forced to stay within it. If they tried to leave, they would be executed.[15]

- All the rules and practices of Islam—such as regular prayers, fasting during Ramadan, or abstaining from alcohol—were also imposed by force. In other words, nobody was forced to enter Islam; however, once they entered it, even by birth, they would be forced to observe all its requirements. Women would be forcefully covered, wine drinkers would be flogged, and even those who skipped their daily prayers would be beaten with sticks.[16]

Is Islam a Kind of State?

That is why, today, when the more liberal-minded Muslims quote the Qur'anic clause, "There is no compulsion in religion," to argue that Islam must be based on freedom rather than coercion, the more conservative ones who are loyal to the traditional jurisprudence immediately object.

One such conservative Muslim is Ahmet Vanlioğlu, a retired Istanbul imam, who gave a passionate sermon in 2017 that was shared on some Turkish Islamic websites with a daring title: "There *is* compulsion in religion!" The popular scholar, who was at the time also the head of a religious foundation, said the following:

> Now, let's say there is someone who does not do his [five-times-a-day] regular prayers. Some say, "How can you force him, there is no compulsion in religion." Well, yes, there is no compulsion *to* religion—but there is compulsion *in* religion. You cannot force a man who is not in the religion to accept it. But there is absolutely compulsion on a man who has entered the religion, who has accepted it.[17]

To justify his case, Vanlioğlu gave an example: Nobody could force you to become a Turkish citizen, if you weren't already. But if you had become a Turkish citizen, then you would be obliged to obey all the laws and regulations of Turkey, and you would face certain punishments if you didn't.

Did he make sense?

Not really, I think, for two reasons. First, most states (except totalitarian ones) would not execute you for "apostasy" when you revoke your citizenship. So if you don't like a state, and you find a better alternative, you can leave it without fear.

Second, states do have coercive powers over you, but those are typically about your obligations to other people (such as you should not steal), not your obligations to God (such as you should pray). States demand lawful citizenship from you, so to speak, not pious worship. For the same reason, they do not care about your sincere intentions (your *niyyah*), which is a crucial Islamic value.

So if Islam was a kind of state, then ideal "Muslims" could even be atheists, as long as they performed all the requirements of Islam perfectly—from praying to fasting—despite having the slightest faith in them.

Yet, alas, the problem we have today is that some Muslims indeed perceive Islam, in part, as a state: a totalitarian one that interferes deeply in individual lives, and also a jealous one that does not let them go away.

Defenders of this view routinely oppose the Muslims who quote the verse "There is no compulsion in religion" to assert individual freedom. "Islam does not believe in this individual freedom," one of them said, "but rather legislates for the individual in his private as in his public life."[18] With the same spirit, Iranian ideologues rebuke Muslims who reject religious policing by saying, "I'm a free person!," "This has nothing to do with you!," or "Don't interfere." Those are misguided Muslims, they say, "with their heads stuffed full of Western ideas."[19]

Are they right about this? Are these yearnings for individual liberty "Western ideas"?

A View from John Locke

Coercive Muslims aren't exactly right here, because individual liberty is not solely a Western idea—it has roots in most traditions, including Islam. But they do have a point: this idea has uniquely flourished in the West, in the past few centuries, with the impact of the Enlightenment. However, they are missing the fact that there was a good reason for it.

That reason was, before the Enlightenment, Europeans had seen the consequences of the fusion of religion and coercive power. Those included the torture chambers of the medieval Catholic Church, where sinners or heretics were tormented, supposedly for their own good. They included "infidels" killed by auto-da-fé, which is public execution by burning people alive at the stake. They also included the Crusades, which shed much blood in the Middle East, and sectarian wars between Catholics and Protestants, which shed even more blood in Europe itself.

As a reaction to all those horrors perpetrated in the name of religion, a certain strain within the Enlightenment developed hostility toward institutionalized religion known as "anti-clericalism," which often mirrored the very oppressiveness it opposed. It was most influential in France, where the long hegemony of the Catholic Church was challenged by a strident secularism called *laïcité*, which still has aspects that curtail religious expressions.

Yet the Enlightenment also had a religion-friendly strain, most influential in Britain and later in the United States, which opposed not religion itself, but its fusion with coercive power.

The key thinker of the religion-friendly Enlightenment was the English philosopher John Locke, often called the Father of Liberalism. In his landmark essay, *A Letter Concerning Toleration* (1689), he argued that states should not impose specific religious doctrines, but rather tolerate them, leaving religion to the realm of the personal conscience and voluntary organizations. And he made this argument thanks to "a radical reinterpretation of the life and teachings of Jesus"—not a rejection or trivialization of it.[20]

For this reinterpretation, Locke first argued—despite the common view of his time—that Christianity itself does not require a Christian state: "There is absolutely no such thing, under the Gospel," he wrote, "as a Christian commonwealth."[21]

Secondly, Locke explained, a Christian state would actually be bad for Christianity. He reasoned that if the state upheld a certain "church," it would also be defining that as the right one.

This view would lead to sectarian tyrannies everywhere, as "every church is orthodox to itself; to others, erroneous or heretical."[22] So if they dominated the state, Arminians and Calvinists, two different strains of Protestantism, would "deprive the members of the other of their estates and liberty," merely because of their differences in "doctrines and ceremonies."[23] Instead of such endless conflicts, Locke argued, different religious doctrines should better tolerate each other, while humbly accepting:

> The decision of that question [true doctrine] belongs only to the supreme Judge of all men [God], to whom also alone belongs the punishment of the erroneous.[24]

Locke's third reason to oppose a religious state was the futility of coercion. The state can never really advance "true religion," he explained, because its "power consists only in outward force," whereas

> All the life and power of true religion consists in the inward and full persuasion of the mind; and faith is not faith without believing. . . . [So], it cannot be compelled . . . by outward force. Confiscation of estate, imprisonment, torments, nothing of that nature can have any such efficacy as to make men change the inward judgement that they have framed of things.[25]

For Locke, in other words, there had to be no compulsion in religion. And to avoid any compulsion, the state had to be religiously neutral. It would be such a neutrality that "neither pagan, nor Mahometan, nor Jew ought to be excluded from the civil rights of the commonwealth."[26]

Locke was planting a powerful seed that would influence many, including the Founding Fathers of the United States. One of them was Thomas Jefferson, who was echoing Locke when he defended religious freedom for "the Jew and the gentile, the Christian and the Mahometan, the Hindoo, the infidel of every denomination."[27]

Yet not all his contemporaries agreed with Locke, whose ideas were "minority views that did not enjoy broad support in seventeenth-century England."[28] Some wrote rebuttals against him. An Anglican cleric named Thomas Long (d. 1707) warned that if Locke's ideal of freedom and tolerance for all is accepted, then it would be "impossible to restrain heresie and impiety."[29] He sounded, in other words, just like some of the conservative clerics or ideologues of the contemporary Muslim world who believe that Islam will be weakened if it is not imposed by force.

A Crisis of Religion

All this means that liberalism isn't irrelevant for us Muslims. Quite the contrary, we are rather at a point in history very similar to that of John Locke. "In much of the Muslim world today, as in Locke's England in the seventeenth century," observes Nader Hashemi, American Muslim academic, "large segments of the population are under the sway of an authoritarian and illiberal religious doctrine."[30] While this doctrine does not include some peculiar European horrors, such as burning people at the stake, it does include others: In Saudi Arabia, people can be beheaded for "apostasy" or "blasphemy," while in Iran they can be publicly hanged, and in Pakistan they can be killed by angry mobs. In the Aceh province of Indonesia, sinners can be publicly caned, whereas in Afghanistan or Sudan, adulterers can be stoned to death.

And, lest we forget, none of these religious dictates are really advancing genuine religiosity. Rather, they are causing two problems that John Locke had also observed in his day. One is "hypocrisy," which I have already touched on: people who are forced to be pious often end up being pious only in appearance, without sincerity in their hearts.

The second problem is what John Locke called "contempt of his divine majesty."[31] It means that when you shove religion down people's throats, those people may end up detesting religion, which is exactly what is happening today in many corners of the Muslim world. From Iran to Turkey and many parts of the Arab world, a new generation of atheists, deists, and other kinds of ex-Muslims have lost all their faith in Islam mainly because of all the oppression, violence, hate, or bigotry they have seen in its name. Their stories—which I have covered in a few of my articles—show that by denying people their natural right to liberty, oppressive Islamic regimes and movements are triggering the greatest wave of apostasy the Islamic civilization has ever seen.[32]

In other words, we have a crisis of religion in the contemporary Muslim world, and at its core lies the notion that there *is* compulsion in religion.

To address the crisis, though, we need to go beyond reiterating "No compulsion in religion." The reason is, besides that short clause from the Qur'an—and some similar verses that seem to support liberty[33]—Islam has a tradition of sacred law, the Sharia. And although the Sharia has a precious aspect that upholds human liberty, some of its interpretations suppress it. The next two chapters will take a look at these two faces of the Sharia, beginning with the troubling one.

2

Why We Need to Rethink the Sharia

> Most Muslims consider the Sharia to be divine. But the only thing that can legitimately be described as divine in Islam is the Qur'an. The Sharia is a human construction; an attempt to understand the divine will in a particular context.
>
> — Ziauddin Sardar, contemporary Muslim scholar[34]

In 2002, a 26-year-old Pakistani woman named Zafran Bibi went to the police station near her remote village in a tribal area to report that she had been raped. Her husband had been in jail for a long time, and the terrible man who abused her was none other than her brother-in-law, Jamal Khan.

The "honor"-obsessed family had first tried a cover-up, but the young woman was finally seeking justice.

Yet what she found was not justice. The police took her to a local court, which soon made an outrageous decision: the woman did not have the necessary "four male eyewitnesses" against the man she was accusing. This, the court reasoned, cleared the man of the charges. But the very fact that she got pregnant without access to her husband was enough proof in itself that she somehow had committed the crime of "adultery." That is why, the court reasoned, Zafran Bibi deserved the grim penalty of death by stoning.

Soon, the poor woman was arrested and jailed, with her newborn in her arms, only to await her brutal execution. Luckily, after public outrage raised by human rights groups and an intervention by the then president Pervez Musharraf, a higher court overturned the verdict and released Zafran Bibi from prison. Yet her life was already ruined, and she would continue to face stigma from her family and community.[35]

All that tragedy was caused by patriarchy and misogyny, problems one may find in virtually any society. But there was also a specific problem in Pakistan's "Islamic laws," which were introduced in 1979 by the general-turned-president Muhammad Zia ul-Haqq. These laws criminalized rape, but not as something separate—and much more serious—than *zina*, the Islamic term for adultery (extramarital sex), traditionally extended to fornication (premarital sex) as well. Instead, rape was defined only as *zina bil-jabr* (adultery/fornication by force). That "force" factor saved the victims of rape from prosecution but did not bring any additional retribution to the rapists, as they were still only guilty of *zina*. In other words, no conceptual difference existed between a rapist who brutalized a female victim and another man who just had consensual sex with his unmarried lover.[36]

Moreover, because of this confusion between adultery/fornication and rape, the evidence required for the former was also required for the latter: testimony of four male eyewitnesses. This extremely high, if not impossible, bar of proof often exonerated the rapists. But their victims could not be exonerated when their "adultery" was proved by their pregnancy, as in the case of Zafran Bibi.

Far worse, Zafran Bibi's tragedy was not an isolated incident. In the decades following the "Islamization of laws" under Zia ul-Haqq, Pakistan has seen more than 2,000 cases of gross injustice against its women.[37] Muslim scholar Hashim Kamali sadly observed the following in 2019:

> Rich landlords abused peasant women and servants, and when the latter complained of rape to the

> authorities, they were themselves punished because they could not find four male eyewitnesses of good character to testify for them.[38]

Why were Pakistani authorities allowing this horror, despite the rightful outrage in the nation, and even beyond? And why were local Islamic courts so obsessed with finding "four male eyewitnesses" in all cases of sexual misconduct?

Why Four Witnesses?

For anyone familiar with Islamic sources, the answer to the second question will be clear: this requirement of four eyewitnesses for sexual crimes comes from none other than the Qur'an. However, when we look carefully into what the Qur'an really says, we see a very different context and a totally different intention.

This context and intention are in the early verses of An-Nur, the 24th *sura*, which were revealed soon after the famous "Necklace Affair" of Aisha, the young wife of the Prophet Muhammad. As the story goes, Aisha joined the Prophet on one of his military expeditions, but on the way back, she was accidentally left behind while looking for a necklace she lost in the desert. Luckily, she returned the next day thanks to a young man who had found her and given her a ride. This led to a rumor in Medina that the two had had an affair, troubling the Prophet and devastating Aisha herself. Soon, however, a new revelation came, condemning "the lie" and those who "concocted" it. "And why did the accusers not bring four witnesses to it?," the verse also asked. "If they cannot produce such witnesses, they are the liars in God's eyes."[39] Another verse legally enacted this strict condition to rule out any future libels:

> As for *those who accuse chaste women [of* zina*], and then fail to provide four witnesses*, strike them eighty times, and reject their testimony ever afterwards: they are the lawbreakers, except for those who repent later and make amends—God is most forgiving and merciful.[40]

In other words, the Qur'an had required four eyewitnesses for any accusation of illicit sex in order to protect women from false accusations—not to protect their rapists! However, centuries later, in Pakistan, the same requirement was exploited precisely to protect rapists, as we have seen.

Exactly how did this horror take place in Pakistan—or Nigeria, where similar cases have also been reported?[41]

One problem was the crudity of the modern-day campaigns of "Islamization of laws," which came out of more ideological zeal than legal prudence. They were carried out so sternly that the leniency factors taken into account by most classical jurists—such as excusing the accused when there is "doubt"—were often disregarded.[42]

Yet classical jurisprudence had big problems as well. First, most classical jurists saw rape as nothing but "*zina* by force," not as a separate and more serious crime.[43] Second, some jurists (of the Maliki school) also considered the pregnancy of an unmarried woman as conclusive evidence of her *zina*, unless she herself proved that she had been raped, which was "a virtually impossible burden for the victim to meet."[44] Third, many jurists "limited the four witnesses in a *zina* case to men"—although the Qur'an didn't specify their gender.[45] Therefore, in the classical age of Islam as well, "women and girls seeking justice against their violators" often faced the "virtually insurmountable challenge" of making their case.[46]

And all these sad facts present us with a broader lesson: the Sharia, the legal tradition of Islam, rises on the most noble intentions—such as the Qur'an's safeguarding of women against libels. But not all the interpretations and implementations of the Sharia have really served those intentions.

The Sharia of the Qur'an

What, really, is the Sharia? The Arabic word literally means "the way." In the whole Qur'an, it occurs only once: "Now We have set you [Muhammad] on a *sharia*, so follow it."[47] The term also has a cognate, where God says to Jews, Christians, and Muslims: "We have assigned a *shir'atan* and a path to each of you."[48] So *sharia* isn't specific to Islam; it is the "way" of any Abrahamic religion.

In this sense, for any Muslim, including myself, the Sharia is God-given. Hence, it is sacred and perfect.

However, when Muslims talk today about "following" or "implementing" the Sharia, most of them go beyond this pristine sense of the term. What they rather refer to is *fiqh* (jurisprudence), which is the human interpretation of the Sharia. This interpretation relies on the divinely revealed Qur'an, but more so on three other sources that all have human imprints on them: First, the *Sunna* (tradition) of the Prophet, largely represented by the hadiths, or "sayings," attributed to him in books canonized almost two centuries after the fact. Then there are *ijma* (consensus) and *qiyas* (analogy), which are methods used by medieval jurists to extract verdicts from the Qur'an and the hadiths.

This surely is a complicated matter. But, in short, I believe in making a clear distinction between the Qur'an and the post-Qur'anic sources. The reason is not only because the latter are more human and therefore less sacred but also because, in the words of the late great scholar Fazlur Rahman (d. 1988), important differences exist between the "Qur'anic worldview" and the dominant post-Qur'anic worldview.[49]

So if we make this distinction and look at the divinely revealed Sharia of the Qur'an, what do we see?

We see that the majority of the Qur'an's 6,236 verses are about God, monotheism, creation, ethics, piety, the afterlife, the struggle of the Prophet, and the stories of former prophets. Only about 100 verses are on legal matters, such as marriage, divorce, inheritance, or contracts. A few of those legal verses are also about what we today call "criminal law." They enact five punishments for five specific crimes:

1. *Qisas* (law of retaliation) for murder and intentional bodily injury—with an encouragement for forgiveness.[50]
2. Amputation of a hand for theft.[51]
3. Execution, hanging, amputation of a hand and foot, or expulsion for *hirabah* (banditry).[52] (The term recently has also been associated with terrorism.)
4. A hundred lashes for *zina*.[53]
5. Eighty lashes for false accusation of *zina*.[54]

These five punishments of the Qur'an (often added with a few verdicts from hadiths) have been enshrined in Islamic jurisprudence as the *hudud* (boundaries) of God, to be implemented without much questioning.[55] In the modern era, Islamist movements often made their enforcement a primary goal, if not an obsession.

However, those Islamist movements seem to be missing three important points.

First, the five Qur'anic punishments do not constitute a fully defined penal code—and neither do they claim to. Rather, they reflect the decadelong experience of the small Muslim community in Medina, to which the Qur'an responded in real time (622–632). That is why the Qur'an also legislated concepts that have no place outside of that immediate context, such as "forbidden months," or *zihar*—Arab customs unknown to other societies.[56]

Second, all Qur'anic punishments have something in common. They are corporal: they cause pain or harm to the body. That has led many Muslims, throughout centuries, to think that, for some mysterious reason, God prefers such punishments to what has become the norm in the modern era: imprisonment. However, we may also think that the Qur'an issued only corporal punishments because, in its immediate context, it was the only way: early 7th-century Arabia had nomadic tribes and little towns with shanty houses, but no state authority to build and operate long-term prisons. No wonder pre-Islamic Arabs also amputated hands for theft.[57]

Third, and the most important point, is that the five Qur'anic punishments target "crimes" in the common sense of that term—they have victims. This is quite clear in the case of murder, theft, violent robbery, and false accusation of *zina*. As for *zina* itself, it isn't often considered a crime today, but if it refers only to extramarital sex—as a few scholars have argued—then it does have a victim, which is the betrayed spouse.[58] Moreover, *zina* can also be condemned for confusing lineage, which was probably the main concern all along, evidenced by the fact that Muslim jurists defined it strictly as genital intercourse, the only kind of sex that leads to reproduction.[59]

Sins versus Crimes

Now, here is the crucial point that relates to our discussion on liberty: besides the five crimes listed earlier, the Qur'an religiously banned many other acts, but it did not legally penalize them. Examples are drinking wine, consuming pork, gambling, lying, gossiping, practicing sorcery, taking usury, looking at someone's private parts, or not fully covering your own private parts.[60] Against all such sins, the Qur'an warned Muslims of God's discontentment and even wrath in the afterlife—but it did not decree any punishment in this world. Similarly, the Qur'an decreed no earthly punishment for Muslims who do not pray or fast, or to apostates or blasphemers.[61]

In other words, we can theorize that the Qur'an made *a distinction between crime and sin*. Crimes were public offenses, such as theft that victimizes people and needs to be punished by people. Sins, on the other hand, were moral offenses that would be left to God. (All crimes were also sins; but not all sins were crimes.)

However, in a few centuries after the Qur'an, this distinction between crime and sin largely disappeared. Scholars who interpreted the Sharia—through *fiqh* (jurisprudence)—criminalized virtually all sins. Accordingly, drinkers were to be flogged and their wine had to be poured out. Those who did not perform their daily prayers were to be beaten with sticks.[62] Apostates were to be executed, unless they recanted in three days. Blasphemers would also be executed, according to some jurists, even if they repented.[63]

It is this medieval jurisprudence that gave us the coercive interpretation of the Sharia, whose champions still insist, "There *is* compulsion in religion." The same jurisprudence also gave more attention to the literal wordings of Qur'anic commandments than the intentions behind them. That is how the requirement of four eyewitness for proving *zina* could be passed on to proving rape, regardless of the disastrous consequences.

The Jurisprudence Post-Qur'an

How did this medieval jurisprudence develop? The question requires a longer answer that I offer in another work, but here is the story in a nutshell.[64]

Because of Islam's emphasis on both religious practice and its early fusion with state power, lawmaking proved to be a crucial matter in the formative centuries of Islam. To this end, some jurists first turned to the Qur'an, but it had very limited legal content, as we have seen. They also respected Sunna, the tradition of the Prophet, but understood it only as "a set of practices and beliefs of the Muslim community as passed on from the companions," in addition to the small number of massively transmitted (*mutawatir*) reports. Then, both to interpret the meaning of the Qur'an and Sunna and to judge rationally even without scripture, they emphasized the authority of human reason. Some were known as *Ahl al-Ray* (People of Reason); others were known as *Ahl al-Kalam* (People of Theology).[65]

Yet other jurists, mostly from more parochial areas, found these rationalist jurists too "whimsical." Instead of human reason, they prioritized hadiths, accepting a much bigger pool of them, despite the fact that generations had passed since the Prophet, and oral reports (and a limited number of texts) about his words and deeds had been mixed with countless hearsays and forgeries. They were called *Ahl al-Hadith* (People of Hadith).

It is the hadith collections of the *Ahl al-Hadith,* who ultimately prevailed thanks to political reasons, that established the basis of most of the coercive rules in Islamic jurisprudence. The grim verdict on apostasy, for example, comes from a doubtful hadith: "Whomever changes his religion, kill him."[66] The same is true for the killing of blasphemers, the stoning of adulterers, the flogging of wine drinkers, the banning of images, or the belittling of women as "lacking in reason and religion."[67] Since the 19th century, some prominent Islamic scholars have challenged the authenticity of such hadiths—and others that seem "vulgar, absurd, theologically objectionable, or morally repugnant"—arguing that they may be later inventions projected back to the Prophet.[68] I agree with those critics—and their forerunners in the formative centuries of Islam—that the hadith literature is an indispensable source of historical knowledge; however, it needs caution in light of the Qur'an, reason, and moral intuition.

But why would medieval Muslim jurists be so fond of establishing coercive rules—either through hadiths or jurisprudential tools? The answer is that coercion was normal in their time and milieu. The empires that the early Muslims faced—the Christian Byzantines and the Zoroastrian Sassanids—all imposed their official religion, with laws that criminalized apostasy, often with the death penalty.[69] Until the Enlightenment, in fact, many Christians believed in the coercive doctrine of *compelle intrare* (compel to enter), which was inferred from a single commandment in the Gospel of Luke: "Compel them to come in, that my house may be full."[70]

Even after the end of outright religious coercion, "moral coercion" survived in Western societies. It was only a century ago that the temperance movement, rooted in Protestant churches, succeeded in criminalizing the production and sale of alcohol in America—only to find out that this prohibition did not help anyone other than those involved in organized crime. And it was only half a century ago that British laws stopped criminalizing homosexuality, hesitantly accepting that "there is a realm of private morality which lies outside the law."[71]

All this means that we can't judge medieval Islamic jurisprudence by today's standards, which would be a mistake. The problem, however, is that some Muslims still see the standards of that medieval Islamic jurisprudence, which reflect the culture of those times, as the divinely mandated Sharia that is valid for all times and all peoples.

A Test of Slavery

To those strictly conservative Muslims, one needs to ask a simple question: What is the verdict of the classical Islamic jurisprudence on slavery?

Unless they represent an extreme fringe, they may affirm, "Islam is against slavery." But if they are a bit informed, they will probably be aware that slavery was justified by virtually all Muslim jurists until the 19th century—when it was abolished, luckily, thanks to both Western pressures from outside and reformists' efforts from within.[72]

Of course, one may argue it was the original intention of Islam to abolish slavery—as seen in the Qur'an's praise for the act of "freeing a slave"—but social conditions matured only in the modern era.[73] This argument—often offered by mainstream Muslim authorities who may be too conservative on other issues—is indeed a good one. But it only opens a wider discussion: If we are acknowledging that it was right to reinterpret the Sharia on slavery, why don't we do the same on other matters? Why don't we, more specifically, also reinterpret all the violent, coercive, patriarchal, or discriminatory elements in traditional jurisprudence?

That is the basis of the much-discussed "reform" needed in Islam today—a reform in jurisprudence, the interpretation of the Sharia, toward less coercion and more liberty. And it will not be a betrayal of the Sharia, but a revival of its spirit in the new context of the modern world.

But wait. . . .

A "revival" of the Sharia? Why would we need that? Why can't we just move on with secular laws and principles?

Some people may ask these questions, especially if they are among the "secularists" of the Muslim world. The reason is that although they may see what is wrong with all the implementations of the Sharia, they may not see anything right about it that deserves any attention. Consequently, they may not see anything wrong with the secular experiments that the Muslim world has seen in the past century—Kemalism in Turkey, Baathism in the Arab world, or the Shah's regime in Iran.

Yet the truth is more nuanced. For besides all its troubling interpretations, the Sharia was also the gatekeeper of a crucial value in the classical Muslim world, whose disappearance had grim consequences in the modern era. So to this other side of the coin we will now turn.

3

What We Should Revive from the Sharia

> One of the requirements for the rule of law is for governments to take their own laws seriously.
>
> — Leon Louw, contemporary liberal thinker[74]

> A certain kind of separation of powers was built into Muslim society from the very start . . . [which] did not need to wait for some Enlightenment doctrine.
>
> — Ernest Gellner, philosopher and anthropologist[75]

In his masterwork *Seyahatname* (Book of Travels), the famous Ottoman chronicler Evliya Çelebi (d. 1682) narrates an interesting story about Sultan Mehmed II, also known as *Fatih* (the Conqueror), for his conquest of Constantinople in 1453. As Çelebi tells us, soon after capturing the magnificent city, the triumphant sultan wanted a similarly magnificent mosque built in his name. For the difficult job, he employed a Greek architect named Atik Sinan, who successfully raised the early version of what is still known as Istanbul's Fatih Mosque. It was an impressive building, but the sultan was disappointed that its dome was lower than that of Hagia Sophia. He took this as an insult, lost his temper, and punished the architect by cutting off both his hands.

The story, so far, seems like a lesson about the misery of the medieval world, where people's precarious lives were at the arbitrary hands of capricious rulers. But there is more to it, as Evliya Çelebi keeps narrating, which adds a silver lining.

The day after he lost his hands, the poor architect went to a *qadi* (Islamic judge) to sue the sultan. The judge heard the case and immediately called on the sultan to give his testimony. "The order is from the Sharia of the Prophet," said the sultan, who wore his robes, picked up his mace, came to the court, and sat down. "Don't sit down, my sir," the judge warned him, though. "Stand up together with your challenger."

Then the judge listened to both sides. At the end, he found the sultan guilty. First, he told him that his obsession with the height of the dome was absurd:

> Vanity is only a disaster, and a low ceiling is not an obstacle to worship. Your stone, even if it is a diamond, is only a stone, but a man, more blessed than an angel, is raised up only in forty years. By cutting his hands, you have acted unwisely out of rage. . . . He has many children, whose maintenance is now on you.[76]

Then, the judge announced the punishment for the sultan: according to the Sharia, he deserved *qisas* (retaliation), which means that he had to suffer the same pain that he had inflicted on the innocent architect. Both his hands, in other words, were to be amputated.

The convicted sultan asked for a way out: instead of facing retaliation, he could compensate the architect and his family. "An amount that would be enough," he offered, "and to be paid from the *bayt-ul mal* [public treasury]."

"No," the judge replied sternly:

> I will not put this burden on the *bayt-ul mal*. This deed has happened without the permission of the Sharia, and the fault is yours. From your own salary [*ulufe*], you need to pay ten silver coins a day.

The sultan said he would even pay 20 coins, as he only craved to be forgiven by the architect, in the sight of God. The architect accepted the offer and the sultan was dismissed.

At the end of the story, Evliya Çelebi adds that the sultan told the judge, "If you had favored me over the architect because I am the sultan, I would have finished you with this mace." In return, the judge proved only more defiant: "Oh my sir, if you did not abide by what I have decreed according to the Sharia, I would have destroyed you with the dragon under my prayer rug."

That dragon, obviously, was only metaphorical. Yet apparently, it was more powerful than the sultan's mace.

What is this story's lesson?

Reading it almost four centuries later, it is hard to know how much of it is historical truth versus pious fiction. But in any case, the story gives us a glimpse of what the Sharia meant in Ottoman society: a law above each and every one, including even the mighty sultan.

A Law above Everyone

All this brings us to the fundamental character of the Sharia that is obvious but too often missed: it was a law that derived not from the rulers, but from a much higher authority—God. Moreover, the people who articulated this law via jurisprudence and guarded it with judicial power—the *ulama* (religious scholars)—were not fully subservient to the rulers. For sure, throughout the complex history of the Islamic civilization, rulers co-opted some of these scholars or encroached on their independence. (And the surge in that encroachment, according to contemporary scholar Ahmet Kuru, was the doom of the Islamic civilization.[77]) Nevertheless, the moral authority of the Sharia never disappeared and it preserved a check on arbitrary power. Noah Feldman, professor of law at Harvard University, explains why:

> The scholars' commitment to the law derived from their understanding of it as God's law, greater certainly than the ruler, but also greater than themselves. The ruler's promise to back up the legal decisions of the scholars with force recognized the formal elevation of law over the arbitrary whims of any one individual. This constitutional arrangement made the law supreme. It established, we might even say, the rule of law.[78]

This rule of law was symbolized in the Ottoman Empire in the office of *Sheikh-ul Islam*, the top jurist, with whom the sultans had to consult—a system that checked some of their excesses. One example was when Sultan Selim the

Grim (r. 1512–1520) wanted to forcibly convert all Christians under his rule into Islam, "to unify the empire within"—only to be stopped by Sheikh-ul Islam Zembilli Ali Efendi, who asserted the Christians' right to preserve their faith.[79] The same jurist also prevented the same sultan from executing a large group of his civil servants, out of mere wrath, reminding him that such punishments could not be given without a proper court decision.[80]

Another story comes from Muslim-ruled India, where the ruthless sultan Alauddin Khalji (r. 1296–1316) wanted to mutilate some officers who annoyed him, and also claimed the public treasury to be his personal wealth—only to be challenged by the top scholar Qadi Mughisuddin. Neither the ruler nor his children have any right to the treasury, Mughisuddin said to the face of the angry sultan. "Whether you send me to prison, or whether you order me to be cut to two," he bravely added, "all this is unlawful."[81]

The point, again, was that the Sharia was above everyone, even the sultan.

Yet not all legal systems had the same spirit. A strong contrast was the tradition of *lex regia* (royal law), codified by the Eastern Roman Emperor Justinian in the 6th century. "What has pleased the prince has the force of law," it read, also clarifying: "The prince is not bound by the laws."[82] The same idea was reflected in the medieval English principle, "The monarch can do no wrong," which itself led to the notion of "sovereign immunity"—a judicial doctrine that prevents the government and its agencies from being sued without their consent.[83] (The United States has a version called "qualified immunity," which gives an "unlawful shield" to law enforcement, as libertarians have rightly criticized.[84])

In the Sharia, however, the notion of legal immunity has been "totally absent,"[85] because no sovereign or official was ever above the Sharia. Just like the Ottoman sultan mentioned earlier, they had to stand up in court in case they broke the law.

But let's stop here and think for a second.

It is nice to recall the legendary stories of medieval Muslim rulers. But today, can you imagine the powerful leader of any Muslim-majority country—such as Turkey, Egypt, Syria, Iran, or Saudi Arabia—facing justice in a court while he is still holding power?

Personally, I can't. At least, I have never seen that in my lifetime. (Conversely, I have seen Muslim leaders facing prosecution, sometimes extremely unjustly, *after* they lose power—but that is the other side of the same coin.)

However, I have seen sitting presidents and prime ministers in liberal democracies in non-Muslim-majority nations—such as the United States, Canada, Italy, and South Korea—being investigated by independent prosecutors, or by legislative assemblies that have the power of impeachment.[86] While I was writing these lines, I also saw the Norwegian prime minister being fined by the police for breaking "social distancing" rules, which was hard to imagine in any Muslim society that I know of.[87]

Why do you think this may be the case? Why do Muslim rulers seem to be above the law now, whereas the law seems above the rulers elsewhere?

What Went Wrong in Islam

The short answer is that, in the past few centuries, rule of law dramatically declined in the Muslim world, whereas it admirably ascended in liberal democracies of the West and elsewhere.[88]

A bit longer answer requires a historical overview, which I can offer through the modern history of my country, Turkey. It began in the early 19th century, when some Ottoman statesmen and intellectuals began to realize that their system, which took the Sharia as sacrosanct, was becoming inadequate to meet the *icabat-ı zamaniye* (requirements of the age). In other words, they realized the need for legal reform. But in most cases, the existing interpretations of the Sharia were too untouchable, and its guardians, the *ulama*, were often "empty of any knowledge of the outside world."[89]

So these reformists found the solution in bypassing the Sharia by expanding the state's authority to issue *kanun* (secular law). Traditionally, it was assumed that the latter could not override the Sharia, but that balance began to shift.[90] When the Ottomans faced the need to accept more religious freedom, for example, they did not touch the Sharia's assumed verdict on apostasy—the death penalty—but in the 1850s, they initiated "a state policy to look the other way."[91] In 1856, they also issued an imperial edict declaring, "No one shall be compelled to change their religion," implying that apostates from Islam would not be forced to recant.[92] By rendering the mainstream interpretation of the Sharia ineffective, one could say, they revived the Qur'anic principle of "No compulsion in religion."

Those Ottoman reforms occurred during the era of Tanzimat (Reorganization), which took its name from the historic imperial edict announced in 1839 by Sultan Abdulmejid II. Novelties included new limitations on the sultan's powers, affirmation of due process in trials, protections on private property, new commercial or criminal laws modeled after those of France, and legal equality for non-Muslims. The latter, especially, was an epoch-changing step, as put later by Halide Edip Adıvar, a prominent Turkish intellectual of the early 20th century. "Down to Tanzimat, the Ottoman Turks had believed that only Muslims could be politically equal," as she wrote. "With Tanzimat they believed that all men could and ought to be politically equal."[93]

This trajectory reached its pinnacle in December 1876, when the Ottoman Empire declared a remarkably liberal constitution. "Every Ottoman enjoys personal liberty on condition of non-interfering with the liberty of others," it read, "without distinction whatever faith they profess."[94] The constitution also established a political system based on the essential condition of the rule of law: "separation of powers," which means the separation of the executive, legislative, and judicial branches.[95]

All these mid-19th-century Ottoman reforms marked one of the brightest chapters in the history of the Islamic civilization—and we will come back to its driving force, "Islamic liberalism," as articulated by the "New Ottomans," later in this book. However, this bright chapter was also cut too short. The constitutional regime announced in December 1876 lasted for only 14 months, to go down in Turkish history as the "First Constitutional Period." In February 1878, the new sultan, Abdulhamid II, used the disastrous war with Russia (1877–1878) as a pretext to suspend the constitution, disband the parliament, and rule despotically for the next three decades.

The Ottoman parliament convened again in 1909, initiating the "Second Constitutional Period," only to soon fall victim to the dictatorship of the nationalist Party of Union and Progress, and the turmoil of World War I. When Ottoman general Mustafa Kemal (Atatürk) founded modern Turkey in 1923 as its first president, his motto was "unity of powers"—powers that would be united in his hands.[96] And when I was writing these lines in 2020, after some intermittent progress, Turkey had collapsed into "unity of powers" again, this time under the Islamist president Recep Tayyip Erdoğan—an ideological answer to, but also a political imitation of, the secularist Atatürk.[97]

In short, the evolution of the premodern Ottoman Empire to a modern state did not work well, if we judge it by the criteria of rule of law and its basis, the separation of powers. That is why American scholar Ruth Austin Miller describes this history as a road that went "from *fiqh* [Islamic jurisprudence] to fascism." The latter term implies the glorification of the state, and the instrumentalization of the law for the interests of the state.[98]

A similar, even darker, pattern has taken place in the Arab world, especially in dictatorial republics, such as Iraq, Syria, Egypt, Libya, and Algeria. The Sharia was bypassed through "modernization," but the latter only helped concentrate all powers—executive, legislative, and judicial—in the hands of draconian parties and narcissist dictators. Their powers were so "arbitrary and pervasive" that "no Arab caliph or Turkish sultan of the past could ever have achieved."[99]

In the meantime, Islamist movements emerged across the Muslim world, calling for the reinstitution of the Sharia. What they meant were objectives such as forcing women to cover their heads, banning alcohol, flogging fornicators, and executing apostates—all the coercive rules I have criticized in the previous chapter. Yet these Islamists had little interest in separation of powers, because just like the secular autocrats they aimed to replace, they wanted to dominate all powers of the state. In Iran, Ayatollah Khomeini elucidated this by a constitutional design, which gave the top jurist—first himself, then his successor Khamenei—absolute power. In this so-called Islamic Republic, "the judicial, legislative, and executive branches of government" were not separated, but rather united as "the instruments of the leader."[100]

At the end of all this authoritarian "modernization," the Muslim world arrived at a terrible point: it lost the main blessing of the Sharia, which is to safeguard rule of law, while it preserved the troubling aspects of the medieval interpretation of the Sharia, which is to impose religion by force.

And in the meantime, the opposite took place in the West, thanks to a better—that is, liberal—modernization.

What Went Right in the West

At the onset of liberalism, much of Europe was a land of absolutism. Kings had "divine rights" to rule, and no Sharia existed to stand above them. "The king is above the law, as both author and giver of strength thereto," as James I of England (r. 1603–1625) put it. So "where he sees the law doubtsome or rigorous, he may interpret or mitigate the same."[101]

That is why, in this absolutist Europe, the power of kings was less limited than their Muslim counterparts. This aspect is reflected in a fascinating letter the French ambassador to the Ottoman Empire sent back to Paris a few years before the French Revolution. The ambassador was asked by his government why the Ottomans were too slow in responding to queries in political negotiations. He responded that the system in Istanbul is different. "Here," he wrote, "things are not as in France where the king is sole master and does as he pleases." "Here," he added, "the sultan has to consult."[102]

One of the critics of those French kings who acted "as he pleases" was Baron de Montesquieu (d. 1755), the philosopher who popularized the term "despotism," only with contempt for it. He found its remedy in *trias politica* (separation of powers), which he defined, systematized, and added to the world's political parlance. The three powers of the state must be separated, he explained, "so that none can abuse power . . . that power shall check power."[103] He deeply impressed the American Founders, particularly James Madison, and also inspired the principles of the United States Constitution.[104] The latter, as Americans are often rightly proud of, established a system of "checks and balances," where the executive, legislative, and judicial branches are separate, so they control and limit each other.

Montesquieu, like John Locke, was one of the founding fathers of liberalism. Both believed in a notion called "natural law." This meant that there are moral truths, discernible by human reason, to "which all men, including governors themselves, should conform."[105] It was their version of the Sharia, so to speak.[106]

Thanks to the advance of liberalism in the past three centuries, arbitrary power in the Western world has been curbed to a great extent. (Terrible alternatives that emerged in the same West—fascism and communism—have fortunately been defeated, at great costs and with great sacrifices.) Meanwhile, the same West also got rid of its own medieval laws that imposed Christianity at the expense of other religions or "heresies." Unlike the Muslim world, in other words, the modern West embraced rule of law, while getting rid of coercion in religion.

That is why since the 19th century, some critical Muslim minds have realized that the virtues they expect to see in the Muslim world are now in the West. One of them, the Egyptian religious scholar Muhammad Abduh (d. 1905), put it poetically: "I went to Europe, and I saw Islam without Muslims," he said, as word has it. "I came back to Egypt, and I saw Muslims without Islam."[107]

To Revive Exactly What?

This chapter is titled "What We Should Revive from the Sharia." It should be clear now that what I mean by that is not reviving the religiously coercive commandments in the medieval interpretations of the Sharia, but rather the Sharia's political function in the premodern Islamic civilization: a sense of law that is above all rulers, a law to which we can hold them accountable.

But what should be the content of that law?

A literalist attachment to the Sharia, the dominant perspective today, will not help us here. We even saw how it can be disastrous, as in the example of Pakistan's adultery laws that required four eyewitnesses for any sexual crime, which persecuted innocent women while protecting their rapists.

Yet that same example also showed us that the Sharia was built on the best *intentions.*

So it is those intentions that we really need to revive.

Fortunately, a scholarly tradition in Islam has already studied those intentions—the *maqasid* (objectives) of the Sharia. We owe this tradition to a few classical Muslim jurists, the most prominent of whom was Abu Ishaq al-Shatibi (d. 1388), a scholar from Granada in Muslim Spain. Unlike most of his predecessors and contemporaries, who focused on the commandments of the Sharia, al-Shatibi focused on the objectives behind those commandments. "Every legal ruling in Islam has a function which it performs," he argued, regardless of whether or not this function is explicitly stated in the ruling itself. He also tied all these functions to an overarching aim: "to realize benefit to human beings, or to ward off harm or corruption."[108]

For example, God had banned and penalized theft to achieve an objective: *hifz al-mal* (protection of property), which itself was essential for human welfare. With a systematic analysis of Sharia rulings, al-Shatibi mapped four more such objectives: the protection of religion (*deen*), life (*nafs*), lineage (*nasl*), and the intellect (*'aql*). In the 20th century, Tunisian scholar Ibn Ashur, who tried to revive the much-forgotten wisdom of al-Shatibi, added a sixth objective: freedom (*hurriyyat*).[109]

It is worth noting here that classical jurists such as al-Shatibi mapped the objectives of the Sharia mainly to defend the Sharia—rather than reinterpreting it—and taking the latter step requires a theological breakthrough, that I addressed elsewhere.[110]

Yet still, even in its classical form, there is something remarkable about the objectives of the Sharia: they are all about protecting the rights of humans—their religion, life, property, lineage, intellect, and freedom. They are *not* about protecting the state, its security, authority, or perpetuity—notions that are easily put above human rights in many parts of the world today, especially in authoritarian regimes, quite a few of which rule over Muslims.

And therein lies the reason why we Muslims need to revive the Sharia—more precisely the spirit of the Sharia. That spirit tells us that rights of humans—that we may establish either by divine law or by human reason—should be above all states, whose legitimacy, if any, derives only from their protection of those rights. And the law, the guardian of those rights, should rule above everyone, including the most powerful rulers.

Yet one may still ask, what would this mean in real life? According to this spirit, what kinds of states should Muslims aspire to? Should we aspire to Sharia-based "Islamic states" or something different?

Those questions require a discussion of the politics of Islam, in addition to its legal tradition we discussed in Chapters 2 and 3. So in the next two chapters, we will discuss some political theory.

4

Will Islam "Conquer" and "Prevail"?

> The world is huge and unconquerable. You cannot cover all the roads you take with leather. [But] you can make shoes for yourself, you can cover your feet with leather, and the result will be the same.
>
> — Alija Izetbegović, Bosnian Muslim intellectual and statesman[111]

Let's imagine that a passenger ship full of diverse passengers sets sail from Europe to America. Unfortunately, something goes wrong in the middle of the Atlantic and the ship sinks into deep, dark waters. At least some passengers survive, though, and some 16 of them are able to reach a deserted island. Once they get over the shock, they gather on the beach to see who has made it. It turns out that among them are three Muslim couples, each husband and wife, in addition to three similar Christian couples. There are also a single Muslim woman, a single Jewish man, and two gay men, one a Hindu and the other an atheist.

As days go by, these survivors build a life on the island. They make huts for themselves, gather vegetables and hunt animals, and also follow their respective religions. Muslims pray toward Mecca, Christians pray to Jesus. Soon, new relationships also develop: the Muslim woman and the Jewish man fall in love and move into the same hut. The two gay men do same—they even announce that they are now happily married.

But things get complicated at some point, as the three Muslim men decide to conquer the island, thanks to their strong muscles and makeshift spears, in order to establish "God's rule"—and Muslim supremacy. After a successful takeover, they tell the Christians that they may keep their religion, but they can't display crosses in public, can't build a new church, and can't publicly drink wine, which one of the Christian couples had begun to make from the island's wild grapes. The Muslim woman and the Jewish man must depart, unless he converts to Islam. The gay men must immediately end their relationship and repent, otherwise they will be first flogged, then executed. Meanwhile, the non-Muslims on the island are welcome to convert to Islam, but if they change their mind again, they will be executed for "apostasy." And every non-Muslim on the island should pay "taxes"—that is, a share of their hunted or gathered food—to the Muslims, who are now the masters.

Now, if you were watching this island from afar, would you think that those Muslim "conquerors" had acted justly?

In case you are unsure, imagine the alternative. The Christians on the island did the same: took over the island by force, "in the name of Christ," to impose on the rest what they believe is the right way of faith and life. Would that be just? Or imagine that the atheist and the Hindu manage to take control of the island and initiate a purge against all "Abrahamic superstitions." Would that be just?

None of these dominations would be just. The same is true even if one of these specific groups on the island is made up of more than half the population and imposed their values on the rest thanks to a popular vote. Because that kind of "democracy" would only mean tyranny of the majority, which is, well, only tyranny.

Here is what would be just: the inhabitants of the island keep living in their own ways, while agreeing on a set of neutral rules they can all live with. For example, those rules could declare that nobody should steal from another, that nobody should interfere in another's religious practices or private affairs, or that everyone should take safety precautions during hunting. Practical, rational rules, so to speak, would allow them to coexist, and even cooperate, without any unresolvable conflict.

For their part, Muslims could see these rational rules as the expression of the *maqasid* (intentions) of the Sharia—the protection of life, religion, property, lineage, intellect, and freedom. Others can substantiate the same values from within their own religious traditions, or mere reason, conscience, and intuition.

This order on the island would not mean that Muslims necessarily approve of all the beliefs or lifestyles of the other groups and individuals. They could still keep their value judgments, even raise criticisms. They would just agree to disagree with the others, so that everybody can live in peace, as they see fit, without anyone becoming hegemonic.

Muslim Supremacy and Hagia Sophia

That hypothetical island, as you may have guessed, is a metaphor for the states of our world. Most of these states were founded long ago, and, unfortunately, on the bad model: conquest. They were founded, in other words, by a certain group of people who used brute force to capture a certain territory and impose their supremacy.

Muslims, who appeared in such a harsh world, also did the same: they established and expanded states, from the early caliphate to the Ottoman Empire, with the power of the sword. Their empires were often relatively tolerant and advanced for their age, but they were still empires formed by invasion and domination, not contract and equality.

Contract and equality were in fact unpopular ideas in the world until they were advocated during the Enlightenment by a few philosophers, including John Locke. In his groundbreaking book *Two Treatises of Government*, in the chapter titled "Of Conquest, and of Usurpation," Locke likened conquest to "a thief obtain[ing] a right in another man's property by taking it by force."[112] Wars would be just, he added, only when they are initiated in the first place by the other side's aggression. Instead of political systems based on conquest and domination, he also proposed what became known as "political contract," where legitimate power comes only from the "consent of the governed."

Such ideas, rough and imperfect at first, led to the rise of liberal democracies and the "liberal international order," which, despite all their flaws and shortcomings, replaced an older order based on brute force. In Western societies, there also emerged self-criticism, even regret, for their dark histories of conquest—such as the premodern Crusades or the modern colonial expeditions.

Meanwhile, in the Muslim world, the era of conquest had long ended. But that was mainly because of the constraints of geopolitics. In theory, the validity of conquest is not much questioned. Quite the contrary: many Muslims have recalled the age of military expansion with "pride and nostalgia."[113] Many of them have also preserved what lies beneath: the idea of a "hierarchical political relationship between Muslims and non-Muslims."[114] It is still a powerful idea in many Muslim societies, where majorities "refuse on principle to be equal with members of other faiths . . . and particularly with those of no faith at all."[115]

I know that idea well from Turkey, where religious conservatives are often proud of "our civilization of conquest," which shows "tolerance" to non-Muslims, but only after defeating them. Hence, on every May 29, they celebrate the "conquest of Istanbul," which was seized from Christian Byzantium in 1453. In July 2020, when they reconverted the great Hagia Sophia church/mosque from a museum back into a mosque, they also celebrated it as a sign of Istanbul's "second conquest," and "the supremacy of the Crescent over the Cross."[116]

That Hagia Sophia affair also created excitement among Muslim communities worldwide. But some Western Muslims had a concern: If they celebrated a "reconquest" in a Muslim-majority nation, which would be an unmistakable sign of Muslim supremacy, how could they keep criticizing white supremacy in America or Europe?

An interesting answer was offered by Sheikh Yasir Qadhi, a prominent American Muslim scholar with conservative credentials. Western Muslims may happily celebrate the reconversion of Hagia Sophia, Dr. Qadhi argued, and without any "embarrassment." The reason, he explained, is that the West has its own religious freedom standards defined by "liberalism," and Western Muslims can "appreciate the freedoms given to us here." Alternatively, Islam had its own standards, which classical jurists had extracted from a purported hadith: "Islam transcends all else, and nothing shall prevail over it." What this means, Dr. Qadhi explained, is as follows:

> Muslims view their faith as being Divinely favored and blessed. Not all faiths are equal, and even if other faiths are allowed to practice and preserve their identity under Islamic law, that does not mean they are all the same. It is because of this that the Sharia has

> many specific rulings for religious minorities living under Islamic law. While there is a lot of discussion regarding the specifics, not a single school of law gave such populations the exact same rights and privileges as those given in the Sharia to believers.[117]

In other words, Islam's claim for religious truth (which any religion may proclaim) also required political and legal supremacy (which not all religions claim). Muslims, therefore, were entitled to establish Islamic islands. They could appreciate civil islands, and their liberal foundations, if they found themselves in it as powerless minorities. But wherever they had power, they could establish supremacy—"clearly and unabashedly," as Dr. Qadhi put it.[118]

But is this double standard really a good idea for us, Muslims of the modern age?

I don't think so.

First, this double standard will be ultimately bad for us. A defense of Muslim supremacy "in the lands of Islam" will only embolden the supremacists in other lands—such as the far-right nativists in the West, or the Hindu nationalists in India. The argument we rightly make against the latter—that the Muslim minority in India should enjoy equal rights—will fall apart, if we deny the same equal rights to the non-Muslim minorities of Pakistan.[119]

Second, this double standard will also be bad for Islam, for a contrast between "liberal" and "Islamic" ways of governance will lead to an inevitable question: Which one of these models is really more virtuous? To rule out the question by saying that one is "manmade" and the other divinely mandated will only convince those who don't dare ask such questions.

Therefore, instead of appreciating civil islands by non-Muslims while idealizing Islamic islands by Muslims—let alone condemning all civil islands on principle, as the extremists do—I believe the right thing to do is to question whether Islam is really inseparable from conquest and supremacy.

And the first step for that is to revisit the heart of the matter: the political legacy of the Prophet Muhammad.

The Political Contract of Medina

Yes, the idea that Islam requires an Islamic state is often traced back, by Muslims themselves or others, to the very founding moment of Islam. Accordingly, in the first stage of the Prophet Muhammad's mission (610–622), Islam was a civil faith in Mecca devoid of any power—just like Christianity it its first three centuries. But in the second stage in Medina (622–632),

Islam enacted its own army, legislation, and taxation, sealing itself as *din wa dawlah* (religion and state).

Yet this popular story has two important blind spots. The first is that the Prophet's mission—as well as the Qur'an that guided it—was "contextual" and "interactive," as I argued elsewhere.[120] In other words, it was a mission partly shaped by the harsh conditions of early 7th-century Arabia, which forced the Prophet, who initially only wanted the freedom to preach his faith, to take up arms. If Mecca's polytheists granted freedom to Muslims, the whole story would be very different.

The second blind spot is that even after his settlement in Medina, the Prophet didn't actually establish an Islamic state. Instead, he established a civil state.

We learn this from Ibn Ishaq, through his student Ibn Hisham, both of whom are the earliest biographers of Muhammad. Accordingly, upon his arrival in Medina, the Prophet was welcomed not only by his Muslim companions but also by some Jewish tribes, which had long lived in the city. The Jews accepted him not as a prophet, but as the leader of Muslims and also a fair arbitrator between conflicting tribes, which was enough for a political contract. "The Messenger of God," therefore, "made a treaty and covenant with the Jews, confirmed them in their religion and possessions, and gave them certain duties and rights."[121]

These duties and rights were simple, but also significant. "The people of this treaty" were declared "a single community [*umma*] distinct from (other) people." It is remarkable that Muslims and Jews were called an *umma*, because the term is used today only for the whole community of Muslims. But apparently the first *umma* was a civil, not religious, entity. Its partners were obliged not to betray each other, and to defend their city-state together.[122] In return, they were free to follow their ways: "to the Jews their religion," as Article 25 of the treaty put it, "and to the Muslims their religion."[123] Another article even affirmed, "Between them is sincere friendship and honorable dealing."[124]

It is also remarkable that the treaty gave little power to the Prophet. As observed by the late Montgomery Watt (d. 2006), one of the towering Western scholars of Islam,

> All that the Constitution explicitly states is that disputes are to be referred to Muhammad. In addition the phrase "Muhammad the prophet" occurs in the preamble. . . . He is very far, however, from being autocratic ruler of Medina. He is merely one among a number of important men.[125]

In other words, in early Medina, the very first state of Muslims, Prophet Muhammad was not an absolute ruler, but a cofounder. The state itself was not Islamic, but civil. And the founding principle was not conquest and domination, but a voluntary contract.

To be sure, this 7th-century contract wasn't identical to the modern political contract theory. It was constituted between tribes and clans, not individuals. But that was the nature of society at that time. Even then, some articles envisioned a post-tribal sense of responsibility. "Anyone who has done wrong or acted treacherously," the document stated, "he brings evil only on himself and his household."[126] (It is in fact remarkable that the modern political contract theory was initially only between the male heads of households.)

The tragedy about this treaty is that it didn't live long. The bloody conflict between the polytheists of Mecca and the Muslims of Medina led to a crisis in Medina. According to the traditional accounts—which now some dispute—Muslims, believing that the Jews were betraying them, purged them, one tribe at a time, after every battle with the polytheists.[127]

So when the Prophet passed away in 632, Medina was dominated by Muslims. Under his *caliphs* (successors), early Muslims began doing what others were doing in their time and milieu: with swords in their hands, they captured large territories and established a vast empire. They tolerated most non-Muslims, but only under a hegemonic hierarchy based on Muslim supremacy—as detailed in the so-called Pact of Umar, which seems to be a later invention reflecting the Byzantine and Sassanian laws of the time.[128]

That is why the Treaty of Medina faded from Islamic memory. Throughout Muslim history, it was not "given the prominence appropriate to an authentic document of this sort."[129] When it was recalled, it was seen only as a stepping-stone to hegemony instead of a civil ideal that could have worked. Only in the 20th century, some Muslim intellectuals, seeking liberal values in Islam, rediscovered the document and highlighted it as "the Constitution of Medina." In it, they had found a "blueprint for a just Muslim polity that treats all its members equally, regardless of religion or creed."[130]

A Choice to Be Made

What does this all mean?

It means that if we seek blueprints in the founding moment of Islam, we can find a political contract based on equality, along with the episodes of conquest, domination, and hegemony.

True, it was the latter themes that the Islamic tradition upheld and established. But this is partly because that tradition itself developed in an age of empires, where conquest, domination, and hegemony seemed to be the natural course of humanity. Yet humanity has come to better standards now, as Muslims living in Western liberal democracies clearly see—and some other Muslims, who are taking great risks to migrate to those liberal democracies, also appreciate.

Hence, it is past time for us Muslims to give up the idea that Islam, through power, will "conquer" places and "prevail" over other faiths. Rather, we should seek ways to peacefully coexist with all other faiths and worldviews, with equal rights and freedoms for all. In other words, we should seek civil islands everywhere, not Islamic ones—which, in practice, even turn out to be the islands of specific interpretations of Islam adopted by self-righteous Muslim sects and groups.

But even when we get to this point, another political question would remain—a question about the internal affairs of the Muslims on our hypothetical island. As a faith community, how would they govern themselves? Could they all be free individuals? Or rather, would they be subject to an internal hierarchy, led by a commander in chief—someone whom they should religiously "obey"?

That is a question that begs another chapter.

5

Should Muslims "Obey" Anybody?

You should hear and obey the ruler, even if he flogs your back and takes your wealth.

— Alleged hadith in *Sahih al-Muslim*[131]

Do not follow blindly what you do not know to be true.

— Qur'an, 17:36

In the mid-1990s, I was a student at the Boğaziçi University in Istanbul. Its famous "middle canteen" was a gathering place for the more ideologically curious students, most of whom fell into one of two opposite camps: the socialists and the

Islamists. I had no interest in the former, but I was seeking my way around the latter, so engaged in many intra-Islamist conversations.

In one such conversation, one of the students who championed Milli Görüş—the ideology of Turkey's main Islamist political party, Refah Partisi—dropped a bomb (metaphorically, not literally). He said that all decent Muslims had to support the leader of his party, Necmettin Erbakan, because he was the *ulu'l amr.*

I knew that this was no small claim, as obeying the *ulu'l amr* (those in authority) is a commandment by none other than the Qur'an:

> You who believe, obey God and the Messenger, and *those in authority among you*. If you are in dispute over any matter, refer it to God and the Messenger, if you truly believe in God and the Last Day: that is better and fairer in the end.[132]

The first two authorities mentioned here—God and the Messenger, the latter being the Prophet Muhammad—are quite obvious, and no Muslim would have any doubt there. However, it is unclear who "those in authority among you" are. Who are they?

For my pro–Milli Görüş friend, the answer was clear: the leader of his own Islamist party. But Turkey had other Islamist movements, some of which were more radical and also illegal, and which considered their leader as the *ulu'l amr*. As I learned more about the Turkish Islamic landscape, I realized that even the masters (sheikhs) of some Sufi orders were considered by their followers as the *ulu'l amr*. A few were even whispered to be the *Mahdi* (the awaited one).

And all this was in the relatively more secular Turkey, where Islamist langue has often been discreet and implicit. In the Arab world, as I discovered over time, the concept of *ulu'l amr* is used in much more explicit ways. In Saudi Arabia, the title is held officially by the king and even the larger royal family. (Saudi Basic Law specifies that *ulu'l amr* means "the rulers."[133]) In Egypt, the draconian president can pass as *ulu'l amr*, as a top jurist put it in 2015. "Whomever obeys President Abdel Fattah al-Sisi obeys the Prophet," he said, "and whomever disobeys him disobeys the Prophet."[134] And in the Islamic Republic of Iran, guess who the *ulu'l amr* is? Of course, it is the top ayatollah, who also happens to be the head of the state, as Khomeini outlined in his doctrine of "guardianship."[135]

While these interpretations equate "those in authority among you" with the political rulers, others transfer the authority to opposition groups. The late Sayyid Qutb, the ideologue of the radical branch of the Muslim Brotherhood of Egypt, made this clear when he interpreted *ulu'l amr* as "believers who stand upon the law of God," which was a reference to the Islamist movement itself.[136] No wonder the Muslim Brotherhood was founded back in the late 1920s on the principle of *'amr wa-ta'a* (obedience without hesitation, question, doubt, or criticism).[137]

In other words, because the Qur'an commands obedience to "those in authority among you" but does not specify who those people are, virtually every Islamic regime or group defines those authorities as their own leader. All of them, one can say, fill in the blank in unmistakably self-serving ways.

A Cascade of Authority

One may think that this is a modern problem, but it has traditional roots, as a quick survey of the various interpretations of 4:59 show. The first interpretation defined "those in authority among you" as the *umara* (political rulers), which surely pleased those rulers, some of whom were bloody tyrants. The second one defined the *ulu'l amr* as the *ulama* (religious scholars), which was a relatively better view as it helped the separation of powers I mentioned back in Chapter 4. But in the words of Turkish theologian Mustafa Öztürk, this second view also led to "*ulama* totalitarianism," where alternative religious views were condemned and suppressed as heresies.[138] Moreover, a third view combined the first two, arguing that the *ulu'l amr* are both the rulers and the scholars, building the "*ulama*-state alliance" that consolidated authoritarian rule in the Sunni world.[139] The Shiites, meanwhile, interpreted *ulu'l amr* as their own imams from the descendants of the Prophet. And in a fifth view, various Sufi orders saw the *ulu'l amr* as their master, or sheikh.[140]

The result of these sometimes-competing but otherwise complementary doctrines of obedience was a cascade of authority, which gave the Muslim individual very little room to think and act on his own. One of the rare minds to criticize—in fact, even to realize—this social control was Ibn Aqil, the 11th-century Baghdadi scholar who was forced by his peers to retract from rationalist views. On the constrained life of the Muslim individual, he wrote the following:

> In infancy he is under the discipline of his parents; when grown up, and in the prime of life, under the restraint of the teacher and professor; and when a mature man, under the restraint of the ruler, unable to dispense with his reform. When will this person free himself from the restraint of men?[141]

The problem, let me stress, was this "restraint of men"—not the authority of God, which every Muslim, including myself, concedes. The problem was that the authority of God was *transferred* to men.

It is worth reminding that the same problem also existed in Christendom until the Enlightenment. No wonder John Locke's first task in his *Two Treatises of Government* was to refute the doctrine of "divine rights of kings," as defended by his contemporary Robert Filmer (d. 1653). Yes, there are God-given "rights," Locke argued, but not to kings to rule over men without question, but to each and every man to live in freedom.

In Islam, a similar view would be raised some two centuries later in the late Ottoman Empire, during the Tanzimat era I mentioned before. One of its champions was Namık Kemal, who had boldly argued that the Ottoman sultan, who also happened to be a caliph, was not the "owner of kingship" (*malik al-mulk*), but only "charged with kingship" (*sahib al-mulk*). So the sultan had to "govern on the basis of the will of the people and the principles of freedom."[142] Kemal also highlighted the Qur'anic notion of *shura* (consultation) to which premodern Muslims had given little attention, but in which he found an inspiration for democracy.[143]

Such views by "Islamic liberals," as they are often called, have helped inspire a certain level of democratization in the

Muslim world since the late 19th century. Yet still, authoritarianism is pervasive and is still supported by religious arguments, which often rely on that vague command, "Obey God and the Messenger, and those in authority among you." (It is also exacerbated by doubtful hadiths that praise the virtues of "obeying the ruler."[144])

So we still need to figure out who those people in authority are. Who are they, really?

A Simple Solution

As I noted earlier, this question has five common answers: "Those in authority" were (1) the rulers, (2) the religious scholars, (3) both the rulers and the scholars, (4) the Shiite imams, or (5) the Sufi sheikhs. These answers obviously differed, but they had something in common: they all assumed that "those in authority among you" must be around us, present in every day and age.

However, one of the earliest Qur'anic exegeses that we know, *Tafsir Muqatil b. Sulayman,* had a remarkably different view: Verse 4:59 was "revealed specifically in reference to the military commander Khalid ibn al-Walid in a particular historical context."[145] That context was an incident where the Prophet appointed Khalid as the commander of a *sariyya*—the kind of military expedition that the Prophet himself didn't lead. But on the road, Khalid had a dispute with Ammar ibn Yasir, another companion.[146] That is why the verse said, "If you are in dispute over any matter, refer it to God and the Messenger." Khalid and Ammar could easily do that, as they did on their return to Medina, because the Messenger was right before their eyes.

Today, however, no Muslim can bring a dispute to "God and the Messenger" in any way. The popular belief that this is realized by referring to the Qur'an and the hadiths is implausible, because these texts can never directly address our current reality. All we can do is find verdicts in them that may have something to do with our current reality—but only by passing through our interpretive lens. That is why disputes among Muslims are hardly ever solved by referring to the Qur'an and the hadiths. How to understand them, in fact, is often the biggest dispute.

For the same reason, there is actually no one who the Prophet may appoint as "those in authority among you." The commanders of the Muslim forces under his authority were clearly his appointees. Once the Prophet left this world, however, there only remained people who could *claim* authority in his absence. No wonder such competing claims soon led to bitter political struggles and even two bloody civil wars among the earliest Muslims.

What should we conclude, then? Who are the *ulu'l amr*?

My answer—in the light of the early exegesis noted above—is simple: they don't exist. There are no such people whom Muslims must religiously "obey." Just like the Qur'anic verses about the Prophet's wives that ceased to be applicable in a generation, Verse 4:59 isn't applicable today. It was a temporary commandment to the first Muslims in Medina who were directly guided by the Prophet who delegated his authority to specific people for specific military missions. But it was not a transmissible authority that could be passed on to whomever claims it, in any age, in any social organization.[147] Otherwise, any Muslim tyrant, populist, or charlatan can claim to be *ulu'l amr*, which is precisely what happens.

That does not mean that Muslims may not have political leaders they recognize and support, or religious scholars they admire and follow. But it does mean that the right relationship between those authorities and individual Muslims is not a military-style obedience that rules out questioning and criticism. Rather, both the political and religious authorities must explain the rationales behind their verdicts, while individual Muslims should be free to make up their minds, and also to raise their voices.

In other words, the Muslims on our hypothetical island deserve to be free individuals. As they don't need to conquer the island, they don't have to enlist behind a commander in chief—the two ideas that are in fact closely connected. Their faith gives them neither supremacy over non-Muslims nor servitude to authoritarian Muslims. So they can manage all their affairs, with everybody, through the democratic and voluntary practices of consultation and contracting.

Yet still, a final question would remain for the Muslims on our hypothetical island: What if they face things that offend them? What if, say, the atheist on the island opens a Society for the Advancement of Profanity, and even distributes some pamphlets that propagate his ungodly views? What if he or other non-Muslims on the island say offensive things about Allah, the Qur'an, or the Prophet?

That question, too, requires another chapter.

6

What to Do with Un-Islamic Speech

[Some] suppose that the more retarded a society is,
the better protected its religion will be.

— Mohammad Khatami, former president of Iran[148]

In the late 1990s, I was a young, aspiring writer in Turkey with a special interest in the science and religion debate. That was partly because, as a faithful Muslim, I was concerned about the scientific atheism proposed by popular authors such as Richard Dawkins. His famous book *The Blind Watchmaker*—in which he used biological evolution to make a case for atheism—had been recently translated into Turkish and had made an impact. As a "theist"—one who is convinced that there is a God—I wanted to figure out the best response and to write about it.

The internet was new then, but it still helped me get a sense of the intellectual landscape on this complex issue and to come to an important realization: all the smart arguments against Dawkins, and other "new atheists," were coming from Western theists—most of them Christians, some of them Jews. Their scholars had published many books, articles, or lectures that advanced "rational theism," which is faith in God defended by reasonable arguments. I devoured all that literature and learned many new concepts—the "anthropic principle" in the cosmos, the "fine-tuning" of natural laws, "the fitness of the environment," the "irreducible complexity" in biological systems, and "methodological" versus "philosophical" naturalism. In the early 2000s, I even helped popularize some of these concepts in Turkey, in op-eds and on TV shows.

But what about our own Islamic resources? We certainly had great Muslim minds—such as Ibn Rushd and al-Ghazali—who also articulated rational theism, but they were almost a millennium old, and most contemporary Muslims just seemed content with reformulating their old arguments. Meanwhile, the new atheists begged for new answers, but much of the Muslim world had already found an easy solution to that problem: shutting them up. Atheist books were unavailable in most Muslim-majority countries, as few would even imagine publishing them. Moreover, being a vocal atheist could land people in jail, get them flogged, or even get them executed in strict Islamic regimes, such as Saudi Arabia and Iran. In other Muslim-majority societies, such as Bangladesh, being an "atheist blogger"—even as an inaccurate accusation—could get people killed by Islamist vigilantes.

Thanks to this easy "solution," so I realized, most Muslim believers never felt the need to defend their faith with reason. Consequently, they didn't produce much that is intellectually significant. In contrast, Western believers, who were living in free societies, had to counter atheist arguments with reason. Thanks to this intellectual challenge, they had become intellectually more sophisticated.

Over time, and with a better grasp of both science and theology, my own ideas became more nuanced—moving from theistic supernaturalism, to put it succinctly, to theistic naturalism.[149] Meanwhile, I dug deeper into the intellectual history of Islam, only to realize something significant. That is, the great Islamic minds of the past that most Muslims revere today were produced by the very challenge that those same Muslims fearfully avoid: exposure to alien ideas.

Bayt al-Hikma and *Majlis al-Munazara*

Islam's exposure to alien ideas began in its very first century, when Muslim conquerors took over centers of ancient civilizations, such as Syria, Iraq, and Egypt, without destroying their preexisting cultures, most of which were Christian. Those Eastern Christians had struggled with complex theological issues, which would soon intrigue Muslims as well. For example, the early Muslim controversy on whether the Qur'an was "created" by God or was "preexistent" with Him seems to be sparked by Christian debates about the nature of Christ. The same is true for the controversy on predestination versus freewill.[150]

Some of these ancient Christian churches had also preserved a precious legacy: Greek philosophy, namely, the books of thinkers such as Plato, Aristotle, Galen, Hippocrates, Dioscorides, and Ptolemy. Muslims soon realized the value of those books and began sponsoring their translation into Arabic, often by employing Christians, initiating what scholars call "the Graeco-Arabic translation movement." It was a world-changing event that "demonstrated for the first time in history that scientific and philosophical thought are international, not bound to a specific language or culture."[151]

This movement had its zenith during the early Abbasid Caliphate—750 to 847—whose marvelous capital, Baghdad, hosted the famous *Bayt al-Hikma* (House of Wisdom), an institute where Muslims, Christians, and Jews worked together on ancient texts. One of its fellows was al-Kindi, who would go down in history as the Father of Arab Philosophy. He was followed by other Muslim philosophers and scientists, who not only studied ancient sources but had their own inventions, making great contributions to European modernity.[152]

A less famous but no less significant institution from the same early Abbasid Caliphate was the *Majlis al-Munazara* (Salon of Debate). It took place in the caliph's court, where intellectual rivals such as Christian theologians were hosted in order to have free debates where every side could speak without fear.

One such encounter that we know about took place in the year 829, when the Abbasid Caliph al-Ma'mun invited Theodore Abu Qurrah, a Christian bishop and theologian from Syria. The caliph seated his guest "with honor in his presence," and posed tough questions, to which the bishop responded with a proud defense of his faith.[153] He even "frequently disparaged Muslims in subtle ways," by calling them "those who claim to have a book sent down to them by God."[154] Then came the most contentious issue: whether Jesus was divine or not. "The bishop demurred," we read in a report of the event, "voicing a concern about his safety should he publicly address such a topic."[155] But the caliph comforted him:

> This *majlis* is fair; in it no one is going to be assailed. Speak your disclaimer; answer without fear. Here there is "nothing but the best." No one will threaten you with anything, nor should you be distressed personally in regard to anyone. This is the day on which the truth is to be made evident. With whomever there is any knowledge for the verification of his religion, let him speak.[156]

The quote in that quotation, "nothing but the best," is from a verse in the Qur'an: "And do not argue with the People of the Book [Jews and Christians] except in a way that is best."[157] During his encounter with Bishop Abu Qurrah, the caliph repeatedly referenced this verse. And apparently, to him it implied a free and open debate without any fear and censorship.

Quite a few such open debates seem to have taken place in the early Islamic civilization. As Sidney Griffith, an expert on Arab Christianity and Muslim–Christian relations, observes,

> One knows from many reports how popular such sessions were among numerous medieval Muslim

> scholars and officials. What is more, there are also reports about how some more pious Muslims in those days were themselves shocked and offended when they attended such sessions for the first time.[158]

It was that shocking openness that made the early Islamic civilization great—leading to the rise of the world's greatest philosophers, scientists, and physicians at the time. Today, Muslims are often proud of that "golden age," honoring it with books, websites, exhibitions, and even dedicated organizations, such as 1001 Inventions.[159] While such efforts are all very helpful, what will be even more helpful is to realize what really explains the stark contrast between that lost golden age of Islam and its grim present: the former was exceptionally open minded for its time, whereas the latter is exceptionally closed minded.

This closed mindedness is quite clear from the extreme limitations on free expression we have in most Muslim-majority societies.[160] Banned books include not just anti-religious ones by assertive atheists but also merely alternative approaches to religion. Even non-Muslim authors who are sympathetic to Islam, such as Karen Armstrong, John Esposito, and Lesley Hazelton, have been banned in Malaysia and Pakistan, only for slightly differing from orthodox religious narratives. My own book, *Islam without Extremes*, was banned in Malaysia between

2017 and 2020—merely for arguing that Islam should not be imposed by force. With such a zeal to ban anything that they find "un-Islamic," or Islamically incorrect, authoritarian Muslims are imposing ignorance on their societies and enfeebling Muslim minds.

That does not mean that nothing can be opposed as "un-Islamic," or that Muslims should not challenge the ideas that they find erroneous. It only means that Muslims should welcome this challenge—as the Qur'an repeatedly says, "Bring your proof!"—and respond with counterarguments.[161] This effort, of course, can be more difficult than banning books and silencing writers, because it requires learning, thinking, and articulating. But these are exactly what we need for a more creative Muslim world. And free expression is exactly what we need to spark that creativity.

What about Insult or Hate Speech?

But what if in a medium of free expression, we face not only intellectual criticism of Islam but also uglier words—such as sheer insult to our religion, or hate-filled words against us Muslims? For some Muslims, the answer is clear: such offensive words must be banned and punished by law. A minority even thinks that if the law is inadequate, then vigilantism should come into play.

With those Muslims, I would agree that offensive words are ugly and there is no virtue or wisdom in uttering or promoting them. If everybody used respectful language instead, the world would be a much better place. However, human reality is more complex and less harmonious. And we are reminded of this by none other than the Qur'an, which, in Verse 3:186, reads: "You are sure to hear much that is hurtful from those who were given the Scripture before you and from those who associate others with God."

This verse was revealed at the time when the Prophet and his followers were settled in Medina—in other words, when they had ample power to silence critics. Yet quite remarkably, the rest of the verse did not command Muslims to silence those "hurtful" words that they will hear from others. It only commanded them to have patience: "If you are steadfast and mindful of God, that is the best course."

Why patience? An interesting answer was given by Fakhr al-Din al-Razi (d. 1210), one of the great Sunni exegetes of the Qur'an. He first noted that some scholars consider this verse to be "abrogated" by "the verse of the sword."[162] But then he added that this is a "weak" view, arguing in contrast that the verse is ever valid. He then reminded of other Qur'anic verses that command patience in the face of enmity—such as God's command to Moses to go to the Pharaoh and "speak to him gently so that he may take heed, or show respect."[163] There are many great wisdoms in such Qur'anic calls for gentleness, al-Razi added, such as "helping the opponents enter religion," or at least calming them down, because "responding to badness with badness only increases badness."[164]

As limited at it was, al-Razi's argument for "killing by kindness"—as I defined it in an article—is one reason why today's Muslims should accept freedom of speech, even in the face of Islamophobic speech.[165]

There is also a second reason, which could not have been imagined by any of our classical scholars, but is now growing obvious in modern societies: if you argue that offensive words must be silenced, you yourself may end up being silenced.

That is because our own Islamic texts—the Qur'an, the hadith literature, and works of classical scholars—also have certain passages that non-Muslims (Christians, Jews, polytheists, or atheists) may find offensive. Some passages may even be seen as "hate speech." We can—and we should—put these harsh texts into their historical contexts, to avoid their extremist implementations. Yet still, those texts exist, and they can well be found disturbing, and even be used as a reason to ban them.

And that is exactly what the Islamophobic movement in Europe is doing. Its proponents—such as the infamous far-right Dutch politician Geert Wilders—argue, "The Qur'an should be banned," pointing to some of its belligerent passages.[166] In return, those who challenge him include true free speech advocates, who remind that "freedom," which Wilders ostensibly defends, means freedom for every view and everyone, including Islam and Muslims.[167]

So, what is the lesson here?

It is that we Muslims need to accept freedom of speech, even when used by some Islamophobes, because we need freedom of speech as well.

This is certainly a new perspective for many Muslims, if not a shocking one. It's no wonder that when Jonathan Brown—an American convert to Islam, a pious Muslim, and a scholar at Georgetown University—defended this perspective in an intra-Muslim conference in March 2020, he baffled his audience and received some angry responses online "for defending those who insult the Prophet." In return, he asked the right question:

> Would you support laws against hate speech or offending sacred beliefs in the U.S. or U.K. that made it illegal to insult the Prophet(s), if those same laws made it illegal to teach sections of the Qur'an or Sunna that talk about other religions, that made

> it illegal for Muslims to teach their children ideas deemed hateful or offensive or intolerant to others? You can't have, and you won't get, one without the other. The choice is yours.[168]

The choice, indeed, is ours, as Muslims. Do we accept freedom, which we need to practice our religion and express ourselves, but which will also set many un-Islamic words free as well? Or just to ban those un-Islamic words, do we prefer unfreedom, which may eventually silence us, too?

The right answer, I believe, is to accept freedom.

And that is not just "in the West," which is the context of the discussion mentioned above. Muslim-majority nations, too, are less homogenous than they are sometimes perceived to be, harboring many different interpretations of Islam, as well as many other faiths and worldviews. A Shiite Muslim's beliefs about early Islamic history may include themes that will be offensive to Sunnis, and vice versa. Even in Sunni Islam, there is a plenitude of different sects, orders, parties, and tendencies. Establishing the sacralities of one of these groups as the truth, while criminalizing others as heresies, will only lead to discrimination, persecution, and even violence, which is exactly what happens in the "Islamic" regimes of our age.

What we need instead are political systems that uphold freedom for everyone—in other words, political systems that accept political liberalism.

Political liberalism is often incomplete, and fragile, however, without *economic* liberalism—an economic order based on private property, free markets, and limited government. Yet today, many Muslims—especially when economic liberalism is denoted with the much-hated term, "capitalism"—think that this is yet another alien idea that contradicts Islam. When we look more carefully into the Islamic tradition itself, though, as we will do next, we may see a different picture.

7

Islam's Lost Heritage of Economic Liberty

> The Islamic economic system is a type of capitalism with a spiritual dimension.
>
> — Muhammad Akram Khan, Pakistani ex-bureaucrat and scholar[169]

> Mediaeval Muslim government . . . was so small that it makes today's libertarian ideal seem like communism.
>
> — Ovamir Anjum, Pakistani-American Muslim scholar[170]

Every year, millions of tourists visit Istanbul's Grand Bazaar, a relic from the 15th century that still hosts some 4,000 shops selling mostly traditional products, such as jewelry, carpets, and silk. Yet not all those tourists, probably, pay close attention to the beautiful engravings on the gates of this great Ottoman shopping mall. One of them, written with golden Arabic letters over a dark green background, reads *El Kasibu Habibullah* (Those who earn are the friends of God).

Who said this? None other than the Prophet Muhammad, reportedly, because this short phrase is nothing but a hadith that has echoed for centuries in Muslim popular culture, especially among shopkeepers.[171] Moreover, it is only one of various hadiths that praise "those who earn." In the hadith collection *Jami at-Tirmizi*, for example, in "The Book on Business," we also hear the Prophet saying, "The truthful, trustworthy merchant is with the Prophets, the truthful, and the martyrs."[172]

Why was the Prophet of Islam so fond of honest merchants? Well, he was one of them. Before the beginning of his Prophetic mission at the late age of 40, the young Muhammad spent much of his life in commerce, which was the most prominent occupation in his city, Mecca. As we know from his Muslim biographers, first under his uncle Abu Talib, then with his first wife Khadija, Muhammad rode in trade caravans to other cities, some as far away as Syria. He made a good profit, as well as a good name, as *al-Amin* (the Trustable).

Not just the Prophet himself but also many of his closest companions were merchants, including those who led the early Muslim community as the first three caliphs: Abu Bakr, Umar, and Uthman. Their tribe, the Quraysh, had long excelled in trade—in fact their very name came from the word *taqarrush*, which means "to come together" and "to trade."[173] So they all knew about business and spoke its language.

It is no accident, therefore, that the Qur'an often uses "the vocabulary of the marketplace both in practical, day-to-day references and in metaphorical applications."[174] The latter include unmistakably commercial expressions, such as Allah "buys" the service of his believers; Muslims are called to give God "a beautiful loan"; those who "barter" guidance for error are unwise; the deeds of everyone will be "weighed" on the judgment day; and the unbelievers will be "the greatest losers."[175] Studying this interesting Qur'anic language more than a century ago, American scholar Charles C. Torrey mapped some 370 verses with "commercial-theological terms."[176]

The same Qur'an defined the Prophets—both Muhammad and his predecessors—as people who "walked through the markets."[177] It warned against fraud in those markets, while approving free exchange. "Do not wrongfully consume each other's wealth," as a verse put it, "but *trade by mutual consent*."[178]

And in its longest verse, the Qur'an instructed Muslims on how to properly write a loan contract.[179]

All such themes in the Qur'an and the Prophet's example have been studied in detail by a diverse set of scholars—from the French Marxist Maxime Rodinson to the German banker Benedikt Koehler—and Muslim economists, such as Murat Çızakça and Ali Salman. They all came up with the same verdict: Islam was born as an unusually market-friendly religion.[180]

"Allah Is the One Who Fixes Prices"

This Islamic spirit is quite clear in the Prophet's approach to the market. As Muslim historian al-Samhudi tells us, soon after Muhammad settled in Medina, he went to an open space, "stamped its ground with his foot," and said to his companions, "This is your market; let it not be narrowed, and let no tax be taken on it."[181] We also know that a few decades later, the despotic Umayyad caliph Mu'awiya (d. 661) imposed taxes on this very first Muslim market—only to be overturned by a more pious caliph, Umar ibn Abd al-Aziz (d. 720), who lifted the taxes and declared the market a "charitable endowment."[182]

Furthermore, the Prophet kept the Medina market free from not only tax but also price control. We learn this from an interesting incident reported in various hadith collections, one of which reads as follows:

> When prices were high in Madinah in the time of Allah's Messenger, the people said, "O Allah's Messenger, prices have become high, so fix them for us." Allah's Messenger replied: "*Allah is the One Who fixes prices*, Who withholds, gives lavishly and provides. And I hope that when I meet Allah, the Most High, none of you will have any claim on me for an injustice regarding blood or property."[183]

This means that the Prophet believed that prices fluctuated according to God's will—that is, beyond human will. He also believed that fixing them by command would lead to injustice. Justice required not a regulated market—as many people intuitively think, both in the past and in the present—but a free market.

Was this a significant insight? Benedikt Koehler, in his remarkable book *Early Islam and the Birth of Capitalism*, answers affirmatively:

> On first blush, deregulating prices in a seventh-century Arabian market for food staples may appear a matter of little consequence. But the economist Friedrich

> von Hayek would disagree. If the price mechanism "were the result of deliberate human design," Hayek averred, "it would have been acclaimed as one of the greatest triumphs of the human mind." When an economy driven by markets rather than by governments comes into being, the ramifications are endless, because taking price-setting out of the hand of government and giving it to the invisible hand of markets has ripple effects on economic incentives—when entrepreneurs rather than officials determine how to allocate resources, economic rationality permeates all spheres of economic life. [Greek historian] Herodotus, Muhammad, and Hayek recognized the importance of the price mechanism to economic activity.[184]

The "economic rationality" Koehler sees at the very birth of Islam did not remain in the birthplace of Islam—the Arabian Peninsula. Soon after the Prophet, Muslims conquered a vast territory stretching from Spain to India, on which they built an empire of faith. They also forged "a monolithic commercial empire that led its merchants from Japan in the East, across all of Asia and Africa, through Europe in the West."[185] In this commercial empire, "powerful *laissez faire* market forces were pervasively at work."[186] The caliphs minted the gold dinar and the silver dirham, providing sound money, and protected both marketplaces and trade routes. Muslim jurists, most of whom were merchants themselves, "accommodated the needs of the merchants," by protecting property, enforcing contracts, and honoring business partnerships, including those between Muslims and non-Muslims.[187] This was major progress in human history, as Islamic commercial laws "set the stage for replacing the 'limited group morality,' characteristic of tribal societies with, a 'generalized morality' consisting of abstract rules applicable to a broad range of social relations."[188]

Consequently, Muslims became "perhaps the most sophisticated business people of the time."[189] Moreover, this sophistication had a big impact on Europe—and not in the way the early 20th-century Belgian historian Henri Pirenne famously argued: as a harmful force that disconnected the Mediterranean from Europe, ruining the latter's urban civilization. "To the contrary," contemporary American scholar Gene W. Heck argues,

> There is powerful source evidence indicating that not only did the Arab Muslims not cast medieval Europe into its early medieval economic abyss . . . but that some three to four centuries later, they provided much of the economic stimulus, as well as a multiplicity of

> commercial instruments that helped pull Europe up from the "Dark Ages" stifling grip.[190]

One of those "commercial instruments" was a solution that Muslim merchants found to counter the risk of carrying large amounts of cash money on long trips. Instead, they began carrying "written documents," or *sakk*, which corresponded to certain amounts of cash. It was soon imported to Europe, where the Arabic *sakk* became the French *cheque*. Tracing the origins of such transfers—including the Arabic origins of *commenda* (limited company)—some historians now argue that Italian capitalism, a precursor to larger European capitalism, was highly indebted to the Islamic civilization.[191]

Ibn Khaldun's Wisdom

The Islamic civilization was also home to a genius who wrote the theory of its economic practice: Ibn Khaldun (d. 1406). He was an Arab scholar who was born in Tunisia and died in Egypt and who was the first to study *ilm al-umran* (science of civilization), the origin of what we today call "social sciences." In his *Muqaddimah* (Introduction) to his larger book on history, he observed what makes nations prosper or fail and found part of the answer in economic activity, whose dynamics he tried to explain.

Modern-day economists who read Ibn Khaldun's explanations are often amazed, because they see "very similar ideas as Adam Smith, but hundreds of years before the Western philosopher."[192] Those ideas include the benefits of division of labor, the law of supply and demand, and the harms of state involvement in trade and production. They also include the fundamental prerequisite of liberal economics, which is the protection of private property, whose wisdom Ibn Khaldun explained as follows:

> It should be known that attacks on people's property remove the incentive to acquire and gain property. People, then, become of the opinion that the purpose and ultimate destiny of (acquiring property) is to have it taken away from them. When the incentive to acquire and obtain property is gone, people no longer make efforts to acquire any. . . . When people no longer do business in order to make a living, and when they cease all gainful activity, the business of civilization slumps, and everything decays.[193]

The "attacks on people's property" could come from banditry but also what Ibn Khaldun repeatedly criticized in the *Muqaddimah*: crippling taxation. "People who collect unjustified taxes commit an injustice," he argued, adding, "injustice ruins civilization." His argument for low taxation would later influence an American economist named Arthur Laffer, as well as an American president, Ronald Reagan, who quoted Ibn Khaldun, repeatedly, both in press conferences and in newspaper articles.[194]

In other words, there is little doubt that the economic system of medieval Islam was capitalism—a "pre-industrial, commercial capitalism," in the words of Turkish scholar Murat Çizakça, who adds, "The West should not have a monopoly over this term." It was a system, in his words, that "favors merchants, respects property rights and free trade, applies the principles of market economy and market wage rate, and treats interference in the markets as transgression."[195]

This verdict may sound bizarre to many Muslims today, for whom "capitalism" is only a dirty word implying greed, selfishness, or exploitation. But those are moral ills that can be found in any kind of social organization—and their darkest examples can be found in communist dictatorships, such as those of Stalin, Mao, or Pol Pot.[196] A more objective definition of capitalism, given by the *Oxford Dictionary of English*, is "an economic system in which a country's trade and industry are controlled by private owners for profit, rather than by the state." By this definition, capitalism seems not just compatible with early Islam, but even characteristic of it.

Yet I should add, Islam's capitalism was also an emphatically charitable one, which commanded—and institutionalized—care and support for the poor and the needy.

The Charity of Islamic Capitalism

One of the earliest emphases of the Qur'an, besides faith rooted in monotheism, was ethics expressed as compassion. The latter had two channels. The first was the obligatory *zakat* (alms), which became enshrined as one of Islam's five main pillars, and also turned (despite some dispute) into a tax collected by the early Muslim state. The second was the more voluntary *sadaqa* (donations). The beneficiaries were defined as "the orphans and the poor," who are repeatedly noted throughout the Qur'an, as well as "relatives, travelers, beggars," and slaves, so they can be set free.[197]

What was the scale of *zakat*? The Qur'an gave no specific measure, but most scholars defined it as an annual 2.5 percent of certain taxable assets, which was a modest levy compared with those in most modern-day states. Moreover, neither the Qur'an nor the early Islamic community decreed any other form of taxation on Muslims. Therefore, economist Timur Kuran sees in *zakat* two implicit values: "personal property rights as well as constraints on government—two key elements of a modern liberal order." However, Kuran adds, later

Islamic empires curtailed this liberal potential by adding much heavier taxes and regulations.[198]

Much later, in the 20th century, *zakat* would be used by some Muslim intellectuals to introduce another novelty to the Islamic civilization: "Islamic socialism." They assumed that Islam's compassion for the poor called for a socialist state that would limit private property and impose massive redistribution. They also relied on a Qur'anic verse warning against "circulation among your wealthy"—despite the fact that it was only about spoils of war.[199]

Yet many other Muslims—including some who experienced socialist regimes firsthand and suffered through their oppression—were not convinced by "Islamic socialism." One of them was the Yugoslav intellectual Alija Izetbegović (d. 2003), a war hero and founding president of his country, Bosnia and Herzegovina, which was the freest Muslim-majority country in the world when I was writing these lines.[200] "Socialism and freedom are not compatible," Izetbegović stressed in his remarkable book *Islam between East and West*.[201] Unlike socialism, he explained, "the goal of Islam is not to eliminate riches but to eliminate misery." This Islamic goal, he added, "does not extend to the equalization of property, the moral and economic justification of which is dubious."[202]

Meanwhile, Izetbegović found *zakat* reminiscent of something else: "the interesting idea of 'negative taxation' as proposed by the American economist Milton Friedman, the Nobel Prize winner for Economic Science in 1976." (The idea was that the people under a certain income would not pay money to the state, but rather would receive money.) As Friedman explained and Izetbegović agreed, this would steer social funds "to those who truly need them, instead of being wasted on inefficient and extremely expensive social services."[203]

I think Izetbegović was right: the Qur'an does not envision a socialist economy, but rather a free economy with institutionalized compassion for the poor and the needy.

Besides *zakat* and *sadaqa*, this institutionalization had a third channel in the Islamic civilization that was also crucial: the *awqaf* (singular *waqf*), which were foundations established by wealthy individuals to finance charitable causes—such as hospitals, soup kitchens, orphanages, mosques, schools, libraries, or monuments. All *awqaf* were established for the sake of God, and therefore they were also protected by the law of God—the Sharia—from encroachment by the rulers. While most were founded and operated by Muslims, Jews and Christians of the Islamic world had their own *awqaf* as well, which were all independent from the state. The whole system reflected "a conservative view of the role of government," where the state was "primarily responsible for security, defense and tax collection, and the *waqf* was a crucial vehicle for welfare support of the people."[204] The state was limited, in other words, and civil society was robust.

The Not-So-Golden Age to Date

Islamic capitalism had its zenith between the 7th and 13th centuries, later to be gradually eclipsed by Western capitalism. But why? Why did the Islamic civilization begin to lose its economic grandeur after a remarkable success?

One common answer is the Mongol catastrophe—an extraordinarily savage invasion, which raised mountains of human skulls—that devastated much of the Muslim world, including its glorious capital, Baghdad, in the middle of the 13th century. Yet some scholars think that even before this external blow, there were internal problems. Political scientist Ahmet Kuru, for example, has recently demonstrated a detrimental transformation in "class relations." While the early Islamic civilization was driven by merchants and independent scholars, in the 12th century,

> First, the military class came to dominate the economy and undermined merchants. . . . Second . . . the Sunni orthodoxy was consolidated and entrenched, while Islamic scholars increasingly became state

> servants. This ideological and institutional transformation gradually eliminated philosophers and independent Islamic scholars.[205]

Consequently, in the long run, Islamic civilization lost its early dynamism and began to stagnate—both economically and legally. Jurisprudence, the interpretation of the Sharia, which had initially boosted Islamic capitalism, failed to adapt to new needs and realities. Until the modern era, for example, it did not recognize the legal personality of the joint-stock company, hindering the rise of what created the economic miracle in the West: corporations.[206] (The same problem—lack of legal personality—also gave most Muslim governments "an intensely personal character."[207])

The result was a sad scene of economic underdevelopment, at the core of which lay lack of economic entrepreneurship. It was regretfully observed by Ismail Gaspiralı (d. 1914), the Crimean Tatar Muslim scholar who spearheaded the *Jadid* (Renewal) movement, in his famous 1907 speech in Cairo:

> [It is] rare to find a Muslim merchant in America or Europe, and if by chance one encountered an Oriental merchant there, he would be Armenian, Greek, Buddhist, Hindu, or Chinese.[208]

To their credit, the Ottomans had realized this problem several decades before and tried to solve it with the structural reforms of the aforementioned Tanzimat era, which began in 1839. Those reforms included free trade agreements with European states, guarantees on private property, privatization of land, new laws for commerce, investments in transportation and infrastructure, and encouragement of the long-lost spirit of Muslim entrepreneurship. The latter was in the mind of Sultan Abdulmejid I (r. 1839–1861), the standard-bearer of Tanzimat, when he introduced the notion of *kumpaniye*, derived from the French word *compagnie*, meaning "company."[209] His wish came true in 1851, when the Ottoman Empire saw the founding of the first joint-stock company predominantly owned by Muslims: *Şirketi Hayriyye* (the Auspicious Corporation), which provided ferry transport between the shores of Istanbul. Five years later, there came another first: the Imperial Ottoman Bank, whose Istanbul headquarters carried that famous hadith, *El Kasibu Habibullah* (Those who earn are the friends of God).

The Tanzimat era reflected an economic policy that can be defined as "liberal," even "libertarian."[210] And it helped raise growth in the Ottoman economy, mainly thanks to the "increasing market orientation of agricultural production."[211]

However, competing nationalisms within and the shifts in power politics abroad brought the Ottoman Empire to a tragic collapse in World War I. This heavy defeat, and the subsequent colonialization of much of the Muslim world, provoked a nationalist response, which found its economic expression in two illiberal ideals: "protectionism" and "statism." The latter—a quasi-socialist model where the state dominates a large portion of the economy—became one of the "six arrows" Atatürk enacted as the founding principles of the Turkish Republic. It included confiscating all the *awqaf*, the charitable foundations of both Muslims and non-Muslims, which once constituted some one-third of the Ottoman economy.[212] "Modernization," in this model, did not mean free markets and civil society, but rather the aggrandizement of a centralized estate.

The same trend was repeated in the Arab world—only often more radically. "Modernization" often implied an overbearing bureaucracy. Most *awqaf* were confiscated—by colonial powers like France in Algeria or by postcolonial dictatorships, such as Gamal Abdel Nasser's Egypt. The latter also spearheaded "Arab socialism," the ideological wave that dominated much of the Arab world in the mid-20th century, only to create "republics" with single-party regimes, ironfisted rulers, and very little freedom, including economic freedom.[213]

Riba, Interest, and "Islamic Economics"

In the late 20th century, another dead end emerged in the Muslim world: "Islamic economics"—an ideological construct that assumed Islam had an "economic system" of its own, with its self-styled rules and institutions.

The centerpiece of this new ideology was an ancient notion: *riba* (increase), a term for a financial practice that the Qur'an condemns quite severely, without clearly defining it.[214] But many Muslims, both in the past and today, have understood it as "all forms of interest," disallowing the very basis of banking.[215] Yet still, in practice, some Muslims realized the rational need for banking. Hence, some Ottoman jurists in the 16th century, despite opposition from more conservative jurists, allowed the so-called cash foundations, which offered "a pre-modern banking system," providing credit with annual interest rates that were, on average, as high as 19 percent.[216]

Moreover, at the end of the 19th century, reformist Islamic scholar Muhammad Abduh broke new ground, arguing that the Qur'anic *riba* was not any kind of interest, but "a specific form of usurious lending that was prevalent in pagan Arabia."[217] Accordingly, a moneylender would give a loan with an agreed time period. If the borrower failed to pay back the loan in time, the lender would extend the term only "with an enormous increase in the principal amount"—or "doubled and multiplied," as the Qur'an described.[218] Therefore,

> The practice in effect led to the multiplication of the debt in the event of late payment, effectively enslaving the debtor to the creditor. [In contrast,] "reasonable" interest, which is more a charge or rent for the use of money, was an acceptable practice if it does not lead to injustices in the creditor–debtor relationship.[219]

Abduh's green light to "reasonable interest" was adopted by some other scholars as well, laying the religious basis for a series of "Muslim banks," which appeared in the early 20th century in Turkey, Bosnia, Egypt, and India. Their aim was to "free up Muslim capital for productive ends" and "to jumpstart a Muslim economic renaissance"—as they really did.[220]

However, the "maximalist definition of *riba*" reasserted itself in the second half of the 20th century, leading to the theory of "Islamic economics," and the practice of "Islamic banks."[221] The latter were different from the earlier "Muslim banks," as they claimed to be "interest-free." But in reality, they only supplemented interest with "labels such as fee, commission, or profit share," and their payments to customers proved "statistically identical to those that conventional banks pay or collect as interest."[222] In other words, they were just modern banks that wore religion on their sleeve.

On the one hand, Islamic banks were useful, as they extended banking services to Muslims who would be otherwise uneasy about them. On the other hand, the trust they gained among the pious was not always well deserved. "Poor oversight by Islamic banking boards with a tenuous grasp of finance," as Timur Kuran observes, "has led to numerous bank failures."[223] A Ponzi scheme in Egypt plundered from more than a million people, while other "Islamic" banks in Turkey, South Africa, Dubai, and Malaysia collapsed because of "lax governance, loans to insiders, or outright fraud."[224] In Germany, more than 200,000 Muslims fell victim to "investment fraud" by the so-called Islamic holdings, which robbed struggling immigrants who only wanted to "abide by the prohibition against interest."[225]

I have seen another disaster caused by "Islamic economics" in Turkey. In mid-2010, after a decade of economic success thanks to pursuing conventional economics and institutional reforms outlined by global markets and the European Union, President Recep Tayyip Erdoğan reverted to his old Islamist ideology. That included a conspiratorial rhetoric about the "interest system," or "the mother and father of all evil."[226]

In the meantime, Erdoğan began pressuring Turkey's Central Bank—whose governors he kept changing, for not being obedient enough—to lower the interest rates of the Turkish lira, promising that it would only do wonders. In reality, the Turkish lira had an "epic downfall," proving to be "the worst-performing currency against the dollar" in the whole world, and creating a "long, painful economic crisis."[227] So while the president kept insisting that "Islamic economics is the solution to the crisis," experts could easily see that it was instead the very cause of it.[228]

Meanwhile, in the same era, Turkey became the global champion in another category: among the top 10 companies in the world that won the largest government procurements, 5 were from Turkey—companies whose bosses were unmistakably very supportive of, and close to, the president.[229] Turkey, in other words, was the world champion of cronyism. And the pious-sounding "Islamic economics" was little more than a fig leaf for it.

The Still-Missing Honest Merchants

Today, out of ideology, dishonesty, or dishonesty posing as ideology, the Islamic civilization has been unable to revive the economic system that once made it thrive—a system of free markets, limited governments, and charitable civil society.

A key component of this modern Muslim failure is the weakness of the driving force behind that early Islamic system—a class of the "truthful, trustworthy merchant" in the words of the Prophet Muhammad, or an "ethical bourgeoisie" in the words of liberal theorist Deirdre McCloskey.[230] Ali Allawi, a former Iraqi politician and Muslim intellectual who pondered "the crisis of the Islamic civilization," also stresses this point. Today, there is certainly a "Muslim super wealthy class," he observes, only to add the following:

> A few of course are genuine businessmen who have made their fortunes by dint of hard work, entrepreneurship and the nurturing of markets; but most have achieved it by the tried and true methods of being proximate to power. Moreover, these people are notorious for their private indulgences and excesses, and their lack of any public spiritedness. There are no major research foundations, universities, hospitals or educational trusts that are funded by large charitable donations. The scale and scope of the philanthropic work of the modern west—especially the US's—is inconceivable amongst the Muslim rich.[231]

The remedy is to make "being proximate to power" less important, so that Muslims see the path to success in merit and hard work, not cronyism and sycophancy. It is also giving up the idea that there must be a self-styled "Islamic" version of everything—just as there is no "Islamic" physics, chemistry, or biology.

There are, rather, objective, universal principles for building economic prosperity, which had worked well in the early Islamic civilization, and recently in the liberal West—and other places that emulated the latter, such as Japan, South Korea, Taiwan, and Hong Kong. These principles—such as "voluntary exchange, competition, personal choice, and protection of persons and their property"—are also summed up as "economic freedom."[232] It is a key aspect of human liberty, which, like other aspects, is desperately needed in the Muslim world today.[233]

8

Is Liberty a Western Conspiracy?

Marg bar liberalism! (Death to liberalism!)

— A slogan of the Iranian Revolution[234]

So far in this book, we have discussed the relationship between Islam and liberalism—in the personal, civil, political, and economic senses. Yet this discussion would be incomplete if we did not address a possible concern: that beneath all such efforts to bridge Islam and liberalism lies a nefarious agenda—namely, to make the Muslim world subservient to "the West" and its imperialist schemes.

This concern is misplaced, as I will argue in this chapter. But it is also quite understandable. The reason is, throughout the past two centuries, Muslims heard the notions of "liberty" or "liberalism" often from the West, which, in the meantime, was often engaged in campaigns to occupy, subjugate, and exploit large parts of the world, including the Muslim world, from Algeria to Indonesia.

This is mainly because liberalism and colonialism largely coincided in Western history in the 18th and 19th centuries. Although not all liberal thinkers supported colonialism, some did, whereas others criticized it.[235] Moreover, the colonialism of illiberal powers—such as fascist Italy, or the communist Soviet Union—was probably more brutal. Yet still, there is enough historical memory to conflate the "liberal West" with the "colonial West."

For worse, Western powers often claimed to be spreading liberal values while justifying their colonial expeditions. In the 19th century, the English called it the "white man's burden," and the French called it the "civilizing mission." Accordingly, non-European nations, which had become "primitive" in the face of Western progress, begged to be saved—and ruled. Muslim women in Algeria, for example, needed to be "liberated" by the French, which ruled the North African nation from 1830 to 1962, often with appalling—say, uncivilized—brutality.

Even before Algeria, the French empire, under the ambitious reign of Napoleon Bonaparte, briefly occupied Egypt from 1798 to 1801, which some historians see as the first big shock Muslims had with Western modernity. Napoleon justified the occupation in a famous address to the Egyptian people, proclaimed in Arabic, where he said, "I have come to rescue you from the hands of the oppressors."[236] It was a line that echoed even two centuries later, in 2003, when American forces occupied another Arab country, with a military invasion dubbed "Operation Iraqi Freedom."

Such snippets of history have made many Muslims, especially those from the colonialism-struck Middle East or the Indian subcontinent, averse to the notion of liberty—let alone liberalism, which sounds like the ideology of the intruder. Even some academics plainly dismiss liberalism as "the National Security Strategy of the United States."[237]

However, these Muslims are missing two important facts. First, while it is true that our forefathers heard liberal concepts initially from colonial Europe, some of them—the first Muslim liberals—used the same concepts to stand up against the same colonial Europe (just like America's Founders, who inherited liberalism from the British, only to launch the War of Independence against the same British). Second, the same Muslim liberals wanted to advance liberty within their own societies, only because they saw it as the secret behind Western success.

We can see these facts right at the beginning of the story, the French occupation of Egypt, which was observed and criticized by Abd al-Rahman al-Jabarti (d. 1822), a religious scholar trained at Al-Azhar University, a beacon of traditional Islamic learning. In his famous book *The History of the French Occupation in Egypt*, al-Jabarti refuted the French claim to advance liberty at the barrel of a gun by showing that the occupation actually did the opposite. He pointed to the unwarranted arrests of Egyptian notables and confiscation of their private property, which he defined as "robbing people of their money by devious means."[238] Under colonial rule, al-Jabarti added, Egyptians "could not travel without a permit (*waraqa*) for which one had to pay a fee."[239] Colonial administrators also "called upon the public to desist from meddling in and discussing political matters," which was again a violation of their liberty.[240] In the words of a contemporary American scholar,

> Jabarti does not describe these events with the terms "freedom of movement" or "freedom of expression," but it is clear that he is using the very concepts that they identify.[241]

Defining these concepts would be the contribution of another Egyptian scholar from the next generation: Rifaʿa al-Tahtawi (d. 1873), another Al-Azhar graduate. During his time, Egypt was under the rule not of the French, but of Muhammad Ali Pasha, a modernizer, who appointed al-Tahtawi as the imam of a group of students sent to France for two years in order to examine the source of European power and prosperity. Here, al-Tahtawi carefully observed "their wonderful government system" and realized the importance of a concept called *liberté*, which did not yet have a clear counterpart in Islamic culture. Hence, he had to explain it to his coreligionists:

> That which they call "freedom," and which they crave, is what we call "justice" (*adl*) and "equity" (*insaf*), inasmuch as rule by freedom means establishing equality in judgements and laws so that the ruler cannot oppress any human being.[242]

Yet a precise Arabo-Islamic term for freedom was clearly needed, and al-Tahtawi coined it: *hurriyat*. The term existed in classical Islam, but only in the sense of being legally "free" as opposed to being a slave. Yet with a "semantic expansion," al-Tahtawi began to use it for political, civil, and economic freedom as well. He also defined various aspects of it, such as "freedom of expression" (*hurriyat al-ta'bir*), "freedom of belief" (*hurriyat al-aqida*), and "freedom of trade" (*hurriyat al-tijara*).[243]

Meanwhile, another term for liberty was coined out of Persian: *serbestiyet* (absence of certain limitations or restrictions). It also had a traditional root but had gained a broader meaning.[244]

These were the sparks that initiated the intellectual movement in the late-19th-century Muslim world that some scholars have called "Islamic liberalism."[245] Its proponents were faithful Muslims who admired Western liberalism and wanted to emulate it—for the sake not of the West, but of the East, and also by finding authentic roots of liberty in Islam itself.

The First Ottoman Liberal: Namık Kemal

The first self-conscious Islamic liberals, in my view, were the "New Ottomans," an intellectual team that gathered in Istanbul in the 1860s to push the Ottoman Empire, through a new profession called "journalism," for more legal reform, political freedom, and ultimately a constitutional regime. They were also the first to offer a synthesis of Islam and "the ideas of the Enlightenment."[246] (They should not be confused with the "Young Turks," a later generation that was less Islamic, less liberal, and more nationalist.)

The most prominent New Ottoman was the aforementioned Namık Kemal (1840–1888), who came from a prominent family and was raised to be a bureaucrat. He instead chose to be an idealist dissident, the cost of which was a short and turbulent life, with several months in jail and many years in exile. He wrote in a series of newspapers, including *Hürriyet* (Liberty), which he published while in exile in London from 1868 to 1869, and in which he sharply criticized the newly growing Ottoman bureaucracy for its authoritarianism and corruption. He himself was a proud Ottoman—in fact, a pioneer of Ottoman patriotism—and he criticized the empire in order to save it. "As long as this tyrannical administration prevails in the state," he warned, "foreign interventions cannot be stopped."[247]

Perhaps the most powerful lines of Kemal were in his *Hürriyet Kasidesi* (Ode to Freedom), a poem published in 1876. It told how he himself fell for the "love" of "the beautiful face of freedom." It also used strong terms, such as *zalim* (oppressor), to condemn certain Ottoman bureaucrats. "This was the first time," as a Turkish intellectual noted much later, "that state authority, glorified in the past five hundred years as that of the Eternal State, was taking a heavy blow."[248]

As I noted before, Kemal introduced into Islam the same transition that John Locke had introduced to Christendom: there are God-given "rights," not to rulers to rule without question, but to each and every individual to live in freedom. "Being created free by God, man is naturally obliged to benefit from this divine gift," he wrote in *Hürriyet*, only to add: "Regardless of time, place, and circumstance, state authority should be realized in the way which will least limit the freedom of the individual."[249] In the words of the late Turkish scholar Şerif Mardin,

> Thus, starting from the premise that freedom was a divine grant, [Kemal] would go on to state that a community (*ümmet*) could be free only when it had been assured of its personal rights (*hukuk-u şahsiye*) and of its political rights (*hukuk-u siyasiye*). Securing personal rights was dependent upon the institution of impartial and competent courts, while political rights depended upon the separation of powers (*kuvvetlerin taksimi*) and the establishment of representative government.[250]

Kemal also advocated freedom of speech, which he observed in "the developed states of Europe," where *ihtilaf* (disagreement) and *münazara* (debate) were seen not as threats to the state but rather contributions. "Such governments are not afraid of criticism," he admiringly observed, "they can be even thankful." Then, with regret, he asked the following:

> Why is this not valid in our state [the Ottoman Empire]? Why is it rather worked for the destruction

> of those who are on disagreement in ideas? . . . Let's assume that the dissidents are not correct in their views. . . . Why, instead of refuting their arguments, is there only enmity shown against their persona?[251]

But was it really valid to borrow ideas from non-Muslims? For Namık Kemal and other New Ottomans, the world was not that clear-cut between Muslims and "infidels." They were rather open to learning from Western sources, which only helped them look back into Islamic sources and find new meanings in them. For example, from the hadith, "the disagreement among my community is a mercy," they inferred the legitimacy of political dissent. They also emphasized the importance of *'aql* (reason) in Islam, in addition to *naql* (textual sources), while connecting the flourishing of reason to freedom. "The spark of truth," Kemal wrote in what would later become an oft-quoted—but little appreciated—line in Turkish political culture, "rises from the clash of ideas."[252]

Namık Kemal was deeply influenced by the political philosophy of Montesquieu, but he was also well versed in, and always loyal to, the Islamic tradition.[253] No wonder one of his latest works, written during a second exile on an Ottoman island, was a rebuttal against the French Orientalist Ernest Renan, who had depicted Islam as "an impediment to the progress of civilization, and an obstacle to freedom of thought."[254] In his bold defense of Islam, Kemal wasn't any less passionate than in his defense of freedom.

Kemal and other New Ottomans—İbrahim Şinasi, Ziya Paşa, Ali Suavi—were able to develop their Islamic-liberal synthesis, in part because they saw Islam as "a set of abstract principles," instead of "a set of concrete practices"—resonant with our discussion of the *intentions* of the Sharia in Chapter 4. In fact, even before them, some Ottoman reformers had begun seeing the Sharia not merely as *fiqh* (jurisprudence), but as an ethical reference against "bribery, nepotism, laziness, apathy, lust for power, oppression."[255] It is that ethical understanding of the Sharia, in addition to openness to the outside world, that seems to have given birth to Islamic liberalism.

The First Tunisian Liberal: Khayr al-Din

Another towering mind from the same era was the Tunisian statesman and intellectual Khayr al-Din (1820–1890). He was born in Circassia and sold into slavery, a trauma that may have planted the seeds of his later affection for liberty. He was just lucky to end up in prominent households, first in Istanbul and then Tunis, and to later win his freedom through a meteoric career in the Tunisian military and then high bureaucracy. He was among the architects of the *Ahd al-Aman* (Fundamental Pact), the reformist program Tunisia initiated in 1857 to secure the rights of life, property, fair taxation, and religious freedom. In 1878, Khayr al-Din would even become the top minister of the Ottoman government, but his advocacy for constitutionalism would quickly displease the absolutist sultan and cut his Istanbul career short.

Khayr al-Din's work also allowed him to live in, and carefully observe, the European society, which inspired his 1867 book *The Surest Path to Knowledge Regarding the Condition of Countries*. "With God's help I have collected all possible information about European inventions related to economic and administrative policies," he wrote, adding that Muslims should be open to learning them, because "wisdom" should be taken "wherever one finds it."[256]

Then he listed all those "inventions" that made the Europeans successful: an elected parliament; a government that is responsible to that parliament; meritocracy in the bureaucracy; promotion of individual success by "granting awards and distinctions to inventors and other creative persons"; libraries open to the public; and joint-stock companies with which he was "fascinated."[257] All these institutions,

Khayr al-Din added, are "based on two pillars—justice and liberty—both of which are sources in our own Holy Law [Sharia]."[258] Then he gave a definition of liberty, which is worth quoting in full:

> The expression "liberty" is used by Europeans in two senses. One is called "personal liberty." This is the individual's complete freedom of action over one's self and property, and the protection of one's person, honor, and wealth. Each is equal before the law to others of the race, so that no individuals need fear encroachment upon their person nor any of their other rights. . . . The laws bind both the rulers and the subjects. . . .
>
> The second sense of liberty is political liberty, which is the demand of the subjects to participate in the politics of the kingdom and to discuss the best course of action. This is similar to what the second caliph, Umar ibn al-Khattab, may God be pleased with him, referred to in saying, "Whoever among you sees any crookedness, then let him set it straight," meaning any deviation in his conduct or governance of the *umma*.

> In addition to this there remains to the public something else which is called freedom of the press, that is, people cannot be prevented from writing what seems to them to be in the public interest, in books or newspapers which can be read by the public. Or they can present their views to the state or the chambers, even if this includes opposition to the state's policy.[259]

Khayr al-Din had economic ideas as well, summed up by the late Turkish thinker Cemil Meriç with a motto: "The best government is the one that governs least."[260] In this, the inspiration came partly from another great Tunisian we have already met, Ibn Khaldun. "According to both the Islamic view and principles of liberalism," hence, Khayr al-Din was able to argue, "the good state was the one which has the least expenses and minimum taxes."[261] Leon Carl Brown, who translated *The Surest Path* into English in 1967, also agreed that Khayr al-Din believed in a limited state. "The state would provide physical security, promote justice and liberty, and that was all." This would "release the creative energies of its subjects, and prosperity would ensue."[262]

But how was it possible that Europeans were so advanced while Muslims weren't? Khayr al-Din put the blame in the Muslim world on "arbitrary rule," and also religious scholars' indifference to the world around them.[263] In contrast, Europe's achievement was thanks to better use of human reason, which led to systems of justice and liberty. To make this argument, Khayr al-Din was relying on a rationalist strain in Islamic jurisprudence, which accepted a "two-sources-of-law theory": that good laws could be based on either divine inspiration or human reason—a universalist view that is still rejected today by Muslim purists who delegitimize any law that is not explicitly Islamic.[264]

A Fateful Turn

The spirit of Namık Kemal and Khayr al-Din was indeed the spirit of most reformers that the late great Arab historian Albert Hourani highlighted in his seminal book *Arabic Thought in the Liberal Age, 1798–1939*.[265] Another towering name from this period was the Egyptian intellectual Ahmad Lutfi al-Sayyid (1872–1963), who embraced British philosopher John Stuart Mill's arguments for free speech and equality for women, while also actively opposing British colonialism and championing Egypt's independence.[266]

Meanwhile, another movement of Islamic liberalism flourished in the 19th century in India, with the works of Syed Ahmad Khan (d. 1898) and his colleague Chiragh Ali

(d. 1895), who advocated modern education for Muslims, along with a new understanding of Islam based on the Qur'an, a critical reading of the hadiths, and a more rational theology.

At the turn of the century, a less known but no less important movement appeared among the Tatars, Turkish-speaking Muslims living under Russian domination: the aforementioned *Jadid* (Renewal) movement. Its key theologian was Musa Jarullah Bigiev (d. 1949), who advocated modern education, participation of women in social life, the revival of *ijtihad* (reinterpretation of the Sharia), and freedom of opinion. The West progressed, Bigiev argued, "through the freedom of reason," whereas "through the captivity of reason, the Muslim world declined."[267]

All these movements in various parts of the Islamic world, in the late 19th and early 20th centuries, were promising trends. Yet as the title of Hourani's book suggests, their "liberal age" came to an end in the second quarter of the 20th century, to be replaced by more authoritarian ideologies: nationalism, socialism, and finally Islamism. What was the reason for this fateful turn?

It is a complicated story, but there is clearly a major factor in it: a series of political traumas.

The first trauma was European colonialism, which reached its height in the aftermath of World War I, when almost all Arab lands turned into British, French, Italian, or Spanish colonies, or "mandates," as they were then euphemistically called. Second, even in independent states, such as Turkey and Iran, secular authoritarian regimes emerged, which were quite different from Islamic liberals, as they were neither Islamic nor liberal. They instead attacked many traditional religious symbols and institutions, including the caliphate, which was abolished in 1924 by Atatürk's new Republican Turkey. Meanwhile, the Jadidis were crushed much more ruthlessly by the Soviet Union, which executed them en masse as "enemies of the people."[268]

The overall result was a deep sense of besiegement of Islam, which only provoked a reactionary Islam. It is no accident that the flagship of Islamism, the Muslim Brotherhood of Egypt, was born right in the middle of this post–World War I shock, in 1928.[269]

Pakistani intellectual Shabbir Akhtar put this turn in a nutshell: "Before the abolition of the caliphate, Muslims wanted to modernize their legal tradition. After its abolition . . . the trend was reversed."[270] Another intellectual from a different perspective, the late American historian Bernard Lewis, also observed the same turn. "The spread of imperialism" in the

Middle East led to "the rise of nationalism," Lewis wrote, adding the following:

> In the general revulsion against the West, Western democracy too was rejected as a fraud and a delusion, of no value to Muslims. The words liberty (*ḥurriyya*) and liberation (*taḥrir*) retained their magic but were emptied of that liberal individualist content which had first attracted Muslim attention in the nineteenth century. . . . [Now,] freedom was a collective, not an individual attribute.[271]

A hallmark of this reactionary political culture, which is still influential in many Muslim societies, was a novelty in the Islamic civilization: conspiracy theory. While premodern Muslims were often confident about their place in the world, the defeats of the modern age, along with real Western intrusions, made many Muslims seek an easy explanation in imagined conspiracies by Western powers and cabals—such as the Elders of Zion.[272] The irony is that this paranoid culture, which built authoritarianism within and animosity against outsiders, also came from outsiders—such as Russian, German, and French anti-Semites.[273] It is no accident that the Turkish term for "conspiracy," *komplo*, appeared only in the 19th century, and as an import of the French word *complot.*

Therefore, we can well say that rather than advancing liberalism in the Muslim world, Western powers in fact often hindered its advance—sometimes unintentionally by exporting their own illiberal ideas, sometimes even intentionally by blocking liberal steps. The latter was the case when European powers showed "a barely-concealed hostility" toward the Ottoman Constitution of 1876, because it would "shut them out of [intervening in] Turkish affairs."[274] A blunter hostility targeted post–Ottoman Syria, in 1920, where a "liberal-Islamic alliance" announced a constitution that guaranteed equal rights for all citizens, including non-Muslims. France and Britain rejected this "first Arab democracy" on the pretext that Arabs were "not yet ready for self-government." A few months later, French armies invaded Syria, ending a much-promising experiment, as historian Elizabeth Thompson elucidates in her significant book *How the West Stole Democracy from the Arabs*.[275]

Muslim Liberalism Today

Let's fast-forward from the 1920s to today. European colonialism is now history. All Muslim nations gained their independence during the great decolonialization wave that followed World War II. To be sure, Western powers—just like others, such as Soviet and post-Soviet Russia—still tried to steer Muslim politics to their advantage, sometimes by orchestrating or supporting coups against elected governments. The United States also occupied Iraq in 2003 with no real justification and repeatedly supported Arab dictators who catered to its interests. All of these Western sins deserve the strongest criticisms, of which there is no shortage in the Muslim world or the Muslim intelligentsia in the West.

However, the history of the postcolonial regimes in the Muslim world (and also post-Westernizing ones in Iran and Turkey) has proved that this world has an internal problem as well: the authoritarianism within. It is a problem that can neither be explained away, nor be helped, by always and only pointing to outside powers.

Quite the contrary, always and only pointing to outside powers helps *sustain* the authoritarianism within, because it often includes the depiction of liberal opposition as a conspiracy of those outside powers.

I have seen how this works in Turkey—and in two different eras. In the 1990s, when I was coming of age, Turkey was dominated by authoritarian secularists (the military and their allies) who despised "the liberals." The latter were intellectuals and organizations that defended the rights of minorities, such as Kurds and Christians, as well as those of the conservative Muslim majority, such as the right to wear a headscarf while attending a university. In return, the authoritarian secularists demonized the liberals as Western puppets, CIA agents, European Union mouthpieces, and payees of German foundations, which all supposedly had nefarious schemes against Turkey. In contrast, conservative Muslims respected those liberals, gave them a voice, and even began considering their views.

But later, in the 2010s when the same conservatives became Turkey's new ruling elite, they also turned authoritarian—quite rapidly and unabashedly—and also turned against the same liberals who were now criticizing them. I personally know people who were purged in the 1990s for defending religious conservatives against oppression, and purged again in the 2010s, only more ruthlessly, this time for criticizing the same religious conservatives for their oppression. And the narrative of the new oppressors was the same old story: liberals were the pawns of a heinous Western conspiracy against our embattled country—and its righteous, glorious, unquestionable leader.

Liberalism has a similar meaning—and stigma—in Iran, as expert scholar Danny Postel observes. First, he explains what "liberalism" means in the Islamic Republic: "the struggle for human rights, women's rights, civil liberties, pluralism, religious toleration, freedom of expression and multi-party democracy."[276] That is why Iranian dissidents, who yearn for those liberal values, aren't interested in "Marxism, poststructuralism, postcolonialism, subaltern studies," which have become dominant paradigms in American academia. They are rather inspired by liberal thinkers, such as Isaiah Berlin, Hannah Arendt, and Karl Popper, as well as the Polish philosopher Leszek Kolakowski, a strong critic of communism, who said,

> There is one freedom on which all other liberties depend—and that is freedom of expression, freedom of speech, of print. If this is taken away, no other freedom can exist, or at least it would be soon suppressed.[277]

Against such liberal ideas, what does the Iranian regime do? It demonizes liberalism and persecutes its vocal defenders, by depicting them as agents of Western imperialism. In the four decades that have passed since the revolution, the Iranian regime has repeatedly depicted liberty as a "Western concept" that only corrupts societies, while demonizing liberals as *ajnabi parast* (foreign worshippers) and persecuting them in its terrible jails.[278]

In other words, the problem in the Muslim world today is not a liberalism that supposedly serves Western imperialism. It is rather native authoritarianism that crushes liberalism by demonizing it as a conspiracy of Western imperialism.

Ideology is at play here; however, there are also mundane interests: for "liberalism" includes the idea that rulers must be held accountable—by independent courts, free media, and civil society—which surely does not please some of those rulers.

One of them was Najib Razak, the prime minister of Malaysia from 2009 to 2018. He was a sworn enemy of "liberalism" and even "human rights-ism."[279] In a major conference with Islamic leaders in 2012, he even declared: "Pluralism, liberalism? All these 'isms' are against Islam and *it is compulsory for us to fight these*."[280] All these sounded extremely conservative, but Razak wasn't really that conservative. When he lost power in May 2018, he was finally arrested for what everybody in Malaysia knew all along: he had plundered a staggering sum of $731 million from state investment funds. That is how he and his wife had acquired a huge collection of diamonds, paintings by Picasso and other great artists, an extravagant yacht, a private jet, and luxury homes in New York, Los Angeles, and London.[281]

Beneath Najib Razak's seemingly purist crusade against "liberalism," in other words, was a murky sea of corruption.

Yet still, in many parts of the Muslim world today, "liberalism" is a dirty word. One reason may be that some people who are called "the liberals"—such as the supporters of Egypt's military dictatorship—don't actually deserve that title.[282] (Being merely anti-Islamist doesn't make people automatically liberal.) The other reason is that "liberalism" is associated with "certain behaviours and lifestyle choices . . . with what one wears or drinks," as Pakistani scholar S. Akbar Zaidi critically notes.[283]

In reality, liberalism is a political philosophy, not a lifestyle. So it would defend a Western-looking lifestyle in the East, as well as an Eastern-looking lifestyle in the West. It would defend freedom *of* religion, as well as freedom *from* religion. It is not a religion, metaphysical worldview, or lifestyle in itself. It is rather a framework that allows different religions, metaphysical worldviews, or lifestyles to coexist, without oppressing each other, and follow their own ways, in peace and dignity, and free of the yoke of all kinds of thugs and tyrants.

Epilogue

I began this book with the story of Muslim women in Saudi Arabia who were forced to practice Islam by abiding by a certain dress code the authorities had defined for them. Their right to be left alone, and to be Muslims in the way they choose, took us to a discussion on liberty with regard to religious practice. Then we discussed some other aspects of liberty—rule of law, separation of powers, political contract theory, individuality, freedom of speech, and economic freedom. I tried to show that while all these values have been better articulated and advanced in the past few centuries in the liberal West, they all had precedents in the Islamic civilization—precedents that *could have been* developed within.

One of those who sees the irony here is a prominent Islamic thinker of our age, Dr. Khaled Abou El Fadl. In a 2020 sermon at the Usuli Institute, he said the following with regret:

> Once upon a time, when the Qur'an told us there's no coercion, even in religion, Muslims were the most forward-thinking, progressive people on the face of the planet. . . . Once upon a time, it was Muslims who were teaching the world the value of freedom.[284]

If we Muslims had kept appreciating "the value of freedom," and systematized it with a political philosophy, we could have also defined it. Instead of "liberalism" (or "libertarianism"), we could have named it with more familiar terms. Perhaps, on the basis of Qur'anic words, *la ikraha fi'l-din* (no compulsion in religion), we could have called it *la ikrahiyya* (no compulsionism).[285]

Instead, we ended up not only failing to do that but also rejecting liberty, dogmatically, because it is supposedly alien, as Khayr al-Din of Tunisia was criticizing some 150 years ago: "Muslims," he sadly observed, were "closing their eyes to what is praiseworthy . . . simply because they have the idea engraved on their minds that all the acts and institutions of those who are not Muslims should be avoided."[286]

Today, it is past time to overcome this parochialism, and to open up to the achievements of humanity, in particular liberty. Because we are paying a heavy price for its absence. We are suffering from dictatorships that kill, jail, or torture their dissidents, sometimes in the name of Islam. We are suffering from corrupt bureaucracies or oppressive communities that do not allow Muslim individuals to realize their God-given potential. We are also suffering from the lack of a free market of ideas, which makes us reiterate the same old narratives, and repeat the same old mistakes. At the extremes, we are even suffering from terrorist groups that bomb the mosque of the "heretical" sect, or kill innocent people of the wrong persuasion.

Liberty, in other words, remains the greatest knot untied, and the greatest dream unfulfilled, in the Muslim world.

Some of our forefathers realized this gridlock, back in the 19th century, and worked hard to open up minds. They were right, and they had an impact, but our trajectory has not yet gone right.

That is why, as a Muslim walking in the footsteps of those forefathers in the early 21st century, by honoring their sacrifices and sharing their hopes, I still defend liberty.

Acknowledgments

I wrote this book during the depressing lockdown of the COVID-19 pandemic in 2020. Hence, I must begin by thanking my wife, Riada, whose love, courage, and resilience in those hard days—while she was also pregnant—contributed to my peace of mind to write.

Then I am grateful to my editor at Libertarianism.org, Aaron Powell, for the very invitation to write this book and the superb editing during the process, along with the key contributions of our colleague Eleanor O'Connor. More broadly, I am grateful to all my colleagues at the Cato Institute, especially Peter Goettler, David Boaz, and Ian Vásquez, who have given me a safe harbor in Washington, DC, to work on Islam and liberty at a time when the world I used to know was turning bleak. That gratitude also goes to the generous donors of the Cato Institute, enabling its principled defense of human freedom since 1977.

I am also deeply thankful to the friends and colleagues who took the time to see my manuscript and made very helpful suggestions: Tom Palmer of the Atlas Network, Javad T. Hashmi of Harvard University, Ahmet Kuru of San Diego State University, Timur Kuran of Duke University, Serdar Kaya of Simon Fraser University, and former Cato Institute interns Yahya Alshamy, Julianne Kelly, and Alex Donley.

What to Read Next

This book is a short introduction to an Islamic case for liberty, which requires a deeper discussion in all the aspects addressed here often briefly. Therefore, I wanted to give a list of other books that may be helpful to the reader for further insight and research.

First, let me recommend my own book *Reopening Muslim Minds: A Return to Reason, Freedom, and Tolerance* (New York: St. Martin's Press, 2021). It delves much more deeply into the theological and philosophical bases of most of the problems mentioned here only briefly. These include fateful rifts in early Islam between the theological approaches of Muʿtazila and the Ashʿarites—one representing "ethical objectivism" versus "divine command theory"—as well as the insights of medieval Muslim philosophers such as Ibn Tufayl and Ibn Rushd, and the little-noticed implications of such precedents on reason to the contemporary discussions on freedom. So if you would like to read anything after this book, I would recommend *Reopening Muslim Minds*.

My earlier book, *Islam without Extremes: A Muslim Case for Liberty* (New York: W. W. Norton, 2011) would be a second recommendation, especially with regard to the 19th-century Ottoman reforms, in addition to a basic introduction to the history of the Islamic civilization from the perspective of liberty. (Only its chapter on Turkey, I must admit, is a bit outdated, as it reflects the hopes I had a decade ago, which only proved to be a sad disappointment.)

Then, here is a list of books by some fine scholars, some of whom have already been referred to in the previous pages, that I would recommend as additional reading:

- For Islamic rethinking on liberty-related issues, see Asma Afsaruddin, *Contemporary Issues in Islam* (Edinburgh: Edinburgh University Press, 2015); Khaled Abou El Fadl, *Reasoning with God: Reclaiming Shari'ah in the Modern Age* (Lanham, MD: Rowman & Littlefield, 2014); Abdullah Saeed and Hassan Saeed, *Freedom of Religion, Apostasy and Islam* (New York: Routledge, 2004); and Fazlur Rahman, *Islam and Modernity: Transformation of an Intellectual Tradition* (Chicago: University of Chicago Press; 1982).

- For critical evaluations of the history of the Islamic civilization, with a focus on liberty, see Ahmet T. Kuru, *Islam, Authoritarianism, and Underdevelopment: A Global and Historical Comparison* (New York: Cambridge University Press, 2019); and Mohamed Charfi, *Islam and Liberty: The Historical Misunderstanding* (New York: Zed Books, 2005).
- For a rethinking of the Sharia and how it can exist under a civil state without dominating it, see Abdullahi Ahmed An-Na'im, *Islam and the Secular State: Negotiating the Future of Shari'a* (Cambridge, MA: Harvard University Press, 2010); and Abdelwahab El-Affendi, *Who Needs an Islamic State?* (London: Malaysia Think Tank, 2008).
- On the relevance of the Enlightenment, in particular the philosophy of John Locke, to the contemporary Muslim world, see Nader Hashemi, *Islam, Secularism, and Liberal Democracy* (New York: Oxford University Press, 2009).
- On women's rights in the Muslim world, and deep-seated problems with patriarchy, see Christina Jones-Pauly and

Abir Dajani Tuqan, *Women under Islam: Gender, Justice and the Politics of Islamic Law* (London: I. B. Tauris, 2011); and Asma Barlas, *"Believing Women" in Islam: Unreading Patriarchal Interpretations of the Qur'an* (Austin: University of Texas Press, 2002).

- On the "Islamic liberalism" of the 19th and early 20th centuries, see Albert Hourani, *Arabic Thought in the Liberal Age, 1798–1939* (Cambridge: Cambridge University Press, 1983); Charles Kurzman, ed., *Liberal Islam: A Sourcebook* (New York: Oxford University Press, 1998); Charles Kurzman, ed., *Modernist Islam, 1840–1940: A Sourcebook* (New York: Oxford University Press, 2002); and Christopher de Bellaigue's not-so-aptly subtitled but well-written book *The Islamic Enlightenment: The Struggle between Faith and Reason; 1798 to Modern Times* (New York: Liveright Publishing, 2017).
- On Islam's free-market heritage, see Benedikt Koehler, *Early Islam and the Birth of Capitalism* (Lanham, MD: Lexington Books, 2014); Murat Çızakça, *Islamic Capitalism and Finance: Origins, Evolution and the Future* (Cheltenham, UK: Edward Elgar, 2011); and Ali Salman, *Islam and Economics: A Primer on Markets, Morality, and Justice* (Grand Rapids, MI: Acton Institute, 2021).

Notes

Unless stated otherwise, all quotes from the Qur'an in this book are from M. A. S. Abdel Haleem, *The Qur'an: A New Translation* (Oxford: Oxford World Classics, 2004).

Introduction

1. Mahmoud Sadri and Ahmed Sadri, eds., *Reason, Freedom, and Democracy in Islam: Essential Writings of Abdolkarim Soroush* (New York: Oxford University Press, 2000), p. 142.

2. Freedom as "the absence of coercive constraint" is a definition offered in Ian Vásquez and Fred McMahon, *Human Freedom Index* (Washington: Cato Institute and Fraser Institute, 2020), p. 3.

3. The statement is from *History of the Party of Labor*, an official publication of the Albanian Communist Party, quoted in James S. O'Donnell, *A Coming of Age: Albania under Enver Hoxha* (New York: Columbia University Press, 1999), p. 141.

4. See "China Portrays Repression of Uighur Birthrates as Victory for Feminism," *Washington Examiner*, January 8, 2021; and "U.S. Says China's Repression of Uighurs Is 'Genocide,'" *New York Times*, January 19, 2021.

5. John Stuart Mill, *On Liberty*, 2nd ed. (London: John W. Parker and Son, West Strand, 1859), p. 22.

6. See Daniel Philpott, *Religious Freedom in Islam* (New York: Oxford University Press: 2019), pp. 177–205.

Chapter 1

7. One may note this Qur'anic verse, 18:29, continues with a threat: "We have prepared a Fire for the wrongdoers that will envelop them from all sides." But that is a punishment to be given by God and only in the afterlife—not a punishment to be given by humans in this world.

8. Reza Afshari, *Human Rights in Iran: The Abuse of Cultural Relativism* (Philadelphia: University of Pennsylvania Press, 2011), p. 8.

9. Qur'an, 2:256 (italics added).

10. Ali ibn Ahmad al-Wahidi, *Asbab al-Nuzul*, trans. Mokrane Guezzou (Amman: Royal Ahl al-Bayt Institute for Islamic Thought, 2008), pp. 24–25.

11. The term "hierarchical tolerance" is from Mohammad Fadel, "No Salvation outside Islam: Muslim Modernists, Democratic Politics, and Islamic Theological Exclusivism," in *Between Heaven and Hell: Islam, Salvation, and the Fate of Others*, ed. Mohammad Hassan Khalil (New York: Oxford University Press, 2013), p. 38. The other point was made by Bernard Lewis: "Second-class citizenship, established by law and the Koran and recognized by public opinion, was far better than the total lack of citizenship that was the fate of non-Christians and even of some deviant Christians in the West." Lewis, "The Revolt of Islam," *New Yorker*, November 19, 2001.

12. In the words of historian Mark Cohen, "The jurisdiction claimed by Islam over the Jewish and Christian communities . . . gave non-Muslims an aura of embeddedness in society. . . . In the economic sphere, the Jews of Islam apparently enjoyed parity with their counterparts belonging to the Islamic *umma*." Cohen, *Under the Crescent and Cross: The Jews in the Middle Ages* (Princeton, NJ: Princeton University Press, 1994), p. 195.

13. Ironically, Jewish and Christian minorities in the Muslim world had their worst periods—and sometimes total destructions—in the past 150 years, due to the new ideologies of nationalism and "anti-imperialism," as well as the radicalization of religious attitudes. See Mustafa Akyol, "Why the Middle East's Christians Are under Attack," *New York Times*, May 26, 2017.

14. S. A. Rahman, *Punishment of Apostasy in Islam* (Kuala Lumpur: Other Press, 2006), p. 8.

15. For a critique of the ban of apostasy in classical Islamic jurisprudence, see Mustafa Akyol, "Freedom Matters II: Apostasy," in *Reopening Muslim Minds: A Return to Reason, Freedom, and Tolerance* (New York: St. Martin's Press, 2021), pp. 195–202.

16. For a critique of these coercive rules in classical Islamic jurisprudence, see Mustafa Akyol, "Freedom Matters I: Hisba," in *Reopening Muslim Minds*, pp. 181–94.

17. "Ahmet Vanlıoğlu: Dinde Zorlama Vardır!" [There is compulsion in religion!], MihrapHaber.com, July 10, 2017.

18. The scholar was the late Ayatollah Mohammad Hussain Fadlallah, who actually had some moderate views on various issues. But even for him, extracting individual freedom from 2:256 was too much. The original quote is in Patricia Crone, *The Qur'ānic Pagans and Related Matters: Collected Studies* (Leiden: Brill, 2016), vol. 1, p. 392.

19. Michael Cook, *Commanding Right and Forbidding Wrong in Islamic Thought* (Cambridge: Cambridge University Press, 2004), pp. 556–57.

20. See Joseph Loconte, *God, Locke, and Liberty: The Struggle for Religious Freedom in the West* (Lanham, MD: Lexington Books, 2014).

21. John Locke, *A Letter Concerning Toleration* (London: J. Brook, 1796), p. 12.

22. Locke, *Letter Concerning Toleration*, p. 21.

23. Locke, *Letter Concerning Toleration*, p. 21.

24. Locke, *Letter Concerning Toleration*, p. 22.

25. Locke, *Letter Concerning Toleration*, p. 12.

26. Locke, *Letter Concerning Toleration*, p. 62. It has often been noted that Locke's tolerance did not fully extend to atheists, whose ethics he did not trust, and even the Catholics, not because of their faith but because of their suspected political loyalties to the papacy. These critiques are obviously valid. But Locke's value is that he opened a way toward toleration, which would mature in time, thanks to latecomers who advanced his ideas.

27. *Hearings*, vol. 5, United States Congress (Washington: U.S. Government Printing Office, 1954), p. 79.

28. Nader Hashemi, *Islam, Secularism and Liberal Democracy* (New York: Oxford University Press, 2009), p. 88.

29. John Marshall, *John Locke, Toleration, and Early Enlightenment Culture* (New York: Cambridge University Press, 2006), p. 449.

30. Hashemi, *Islam, Secularism and Liberal Democracy*, p. 69. The original sentence in the book is restructured here with the author's permission.

31. Locke mentions both "hypocrisy" and "contempt" in *A Letter Concerning Toleration*, p. 12.

32. See Mustafa Akyol, "How Islamists Are Ruining Islam," in *Current Trends in Islamist Ideology*, vol. 26 (Washington: Hudson Institute, 2020), pp. 5–19; and Mustafa Akyol, "How Islamism Drives Muslims to Convert," *New York Times*, March 25, 2018.

33. Some of those Qur'anic verses that seem supportive of freedom are 5:48, 6:35, 6:104, 6:107, 10:99, 18:19, and 109:6. For an evaluation of these verses, see Mustafa Akyol, "What Islam Initially Asked For," in *Reopening Muslim Minds*, pp. 166–96.

Chapter 2

34. Ziauddin Sardar, interview by Mustafa Nazir Ahmad, *News on Sunday*, Karachi, November 23, 2008.

35. "Sentenced to Death, Rape Victim Is Freed by Pakistani Court," *New York Times*, June 8, 2002.

36. For a summary of Pakistan's history with rape laws, see Maliha Zia Lari, "Rape Laws in Pakistan: A History of Injustice," *The Dawn*, March 30, 2014.

37. For some of these cases, see Moeen H. Cheema, "Cases and Controversies: Pregnancy as Proof of Guilt under Pakistan's Hudood Laws," *Brooklyn Journal of International Law* 32, no. 1 (2006): 121–60. Mohammad Hashim Kamali notes that the number of unjustly jailed women in Pakistan was at some point more than 2,000. Kamali, *Crime and Punishment in Islamic Law: A Fresh Interpretation* (New York: Oxford University Press, 2019), p. 247.

38. Kamali, *Crime and Punishment in Islamic Law*, p. 247.

39. Qur'an, 24:10–13.

40. Qur'an, 24:4–5 (italics added).

41. Chineze J. Onyejekwe, "Nigeria: The Dominance of Rape," *Journal of International Women's Studies* 10, no. 1 (2008): 53. According to the author, "The way current Sharia laws [in Nigeria] are framed make it virtually impossible to prosecute rape," because of "the burden of proof that courts place on a victim."

42. See Intisar A. Rabb, *Doubt in Islamic Law: A History of Legal Maxims, Interpretation, and Islamic Criminal Law* (New York: Cambridge University Press, 2015), pp. 115–20. Hina Azam also agrees that a specific Maliki problem—taking pregnancy as conclusive evidence of *zina*—has unfortunately been adopted by most contemporary "Islamic" legal systems, which made things typically worse by conjoining "the most problematic and gender discriminatory aspects of the Hanafi and Maliki approaches." Azam, *Sexual Violation in Islamic Law: Substance, Evidence, and Procedure* (Cambridge: Cambridge University Press, 2017), pp. 243–44.

43. Azman Mohd Noor, "Problem of Crime Classification in Islamic Law," *Arab Law Quarterly* 24, no. 4 (2010): 427–33. As Noor mentions in this article, only a few classical jurists considered rape as *hirabah* (violent robbery), which is a more serious crime than adultery, and this view has gained more popularity in the modern era.

44. Kamali, *Crime and Punishment in Islamic Law*, p. 68; and Rabb, *Doubt in Islamic Law*, p. 159.

45. Asifa Quraishi, "Her Honor: An Islamic Critique of the Rape Laws of Pakistan from a Woman-Sensitive Perspective," *Michigan Journal of International Law* 18, no. 2 (1997): 305.

46. Azam, *Sexual Violation in Islamic Law,* p. 170. Azam makes this comment specifically for the Hanafi school, which considered rape a "violation against God," rather than "a dual violation against both God and a human victim." Intisar A. Rabb observes the same problem in the Maliki school, adding that, in general, "in Islamic law contexts rape was notoriously hard to prove." Rabb, *Doubt in Islamic Law,* p. 15.

47. Qur'an, 45:18.

48. Qur'an, 5:48.

49. See Fazlur Rahman, *Islam and Modernity: The Transformation of an Intellectual Tradition* (Chicago: University of Chicago Press, 1982), pp. 3–4. Here, Fazlur Rahman uses the term "Qur'anic *weltanschauung,*" which I translated as "Qur'anic worldview." He contrasts this Qur'anic worldview mainly with "Ash'arism, the dominant Sunni theology throughout medieval Islam." For an extensive critique of Ash'arism, see Mustafa Akyol, *Reopening Muslim Minds.*

50. Qur'an, 2:178.

51. Qur'an, 5:38.

52. Qur'an, 5:33.

53. Qur'an, 24:2.

54. Qur'an, 24:4.

55. Interestingly, *qisas* isn't always listed among the *hudud,* as it comes with an option of forgiveness. Meanwhile, non-Qur'anic *hudud*—such as execution for apostasy and flogging for drinking—have been extracted from the hadiths.

56. "Forbidden months" were four consecutive months in the Arab lunar calendar—Rajab, Dhu al-Qa'dah, Dhu al-Hijjah, and Muharram—during which war was banned so people could travel for pilgrimage. This preexisting Arab custom was honored by the Qur'an (in 2:217, 2:194, 5:2, 5:97, 9:5, and 9:36) but was largely forgotten by later Islamic jurisprudence that grew in a context where the notion was neither known nor functional. *Zihar,* another pre-Islamic Arab custom, was an act of instant and unilateral divorce by men—by saying to their wives, "You are like my mother"—which is disapproved by the Qur'an in 33:4 and 58:2–3.

57. The Qur'an contains a verse about detention in homes (4:15) and there are some narrations about short-term detainment of criminals or prisoners of war, but they do not refer to formal prisons, and these detainments "were not main punishments, but temporary measures such as arrest until the verdict." Ali Bardakoğlu, "Hapis," *İslam Ansiklopedisi* (Istanbul: Türkiye Diyanet Vakfı, 1997), vol. 16, p. 55. For more of this argument, see Mustafa Akyol, *Reopening Muslim Minds*, pp. 169–72.

58. The Quranic term for adultery, *zina*, is defined by neither the Qur'an itself nor the hadiths, whereas Islamic tradition took it to mean both premarital and extramarital sex. However, a case can be made that it refers only to extramarital sex. A hadith reads that it is a grave sin to "commit *zina* with the wife of your neighbor," suggesting that *zina* is something done with a married woman. *Sahih Muslim*, "Kitab al-Iman," hadiths 156 and 157. According to such indicators, Islamic scholars Muhammad Abduh and Rashid Rida argued that "the punishment of *zina* is only applicable to offenders who were parties to a valid marriage at the time of committing the offence." Kamali, *Crime and Punishment in Islamic Law*, p. 76.

59. Islamic scholars have almost agreed that *zina* is the intercourse of male and female sex organs, in a way that they "meet like the kohl needle entering the kohl bottle." On the basis of this argument, Hanafi scholars excluded homosexuality from the definition of *zina*. Azam, *Sexual Violation in Islamic Law*, pp. 171–72. This does not mean that other forms of sexuality other than *zina* were religiously approved. Virtually all nonmarital sex has been defined as sinful, yet not necessarily as *zina*, which is defined as a criminal act.

60. Qur'an, 2:102, 2:278, 5:3, 5:90–91, 22:30, 24:30, 24:31, 49:12.

61. See Mustafa Akyol, "The Freedom to Sin," in *Islam without Extremes: A Muslim Case for Liberty* (New York: W. W. Norton, 2011), pp. 262–72.

62. For an example, see a classic manual of Hanafi law: Hasan Shurunbulali, *Nur al-Idah: The Light of Clarification*, trans. Wesam Charkawi (Damascus, 2007), p. 200: "The one who intentionally neglects prayer due to laziness or idleness, is to be beaten harshly until blood flows from his body and is then imprisoned

during which he is subject to physical pain, until he performs his prayers or dies in confinement. This ruling also applies for one who does not fast [in] Ramadan due to laziness."

63. See Mustafa Akyol, "Freedom Matters III: Blasphemy" in *Reopening Muslim Minds*, p. 206.

64. See Mustafa Akyol, "How the Sharia Stagnated" in *Reopening Muslim Minds*, pp. 72–85.

65. Jonathan A. C. Brown, *Hadith: Muhammad's Legacy in the Medieval and Modern World* (London: Oneworld Publications, 2009), pp. 151–52. *Ahl al-Ray* is a reference mainly to early Hanafis, whereas *Ahl al-Kalam* is a reference to the Muʿtazila.

66. *Sahih al-Bukhari*, Book 88, Hadith 5. The same hadith, with slight variations, also exists in other major hadith collections, such as that of *Sunan an-Nasa'i*, *Jami at-Tirmidhi*, and *Sunan ibn Majah*. For an evaluation of their authenticity, see Mustafa Akyol, "Two Suspicious Hadiths," in *Reopening Muslim Minds*, pp. 197–99.

67. Hadiths relating to such verdicts can be found in various volumes of the canonical collections of the Sunni tradition. For killing of blasphemers, see *Sunan Abi Dawud*, no. 4362; for stoning of adulterers, see *Sahih al-Bukhari*, no. 3635; for flogging of wine drinkers (and ultimately killing them), see *Sunan Abi Dawud*, no. 4482; for banning images, see *Jami at-Tirmidhi*, no. 1749; and for the defining of women as "lacking in reason and religion," see *Sunan Abi Dawud*, no. 4679. On the latter issue, also see Hidayet Şefkatli Tuksal, "Misogynistic Reports in the Hadith Literature," in *Muslima Theology: The Voices of Muslim Women Theologians*, ed. Ednan Aslan, Marcia Hermansen, and Elif Medeni (Frankfurt: Peter Lang AG, 2013), pp. 133–54.

68. The quotation is a summary of the views of modern-day Muslim hadith critics. Daniel Brown, *Rethinking Tradition in Modern Islamic Thought* (Cambridge: Cambridge University Press, 1999), p. 95. Some of those scholars or public intellectuals are Syed Ahmad Khan, Muhammad Abduh, Rashid Rida, Mehmed Akif, Musa Jarullah Bigiev, Ahmad Amin, Ghulam Ahmed Parvez, Muhammad Tawfiq Sidqi, İzmirli İsmail Hakkı, Aksekili Ahmed Hamdi, Mahmud Abu Rayya, Mohammed al-Ghazali, Fazlur Rahman Malik, and Javed Ahmed Ghamidi.

69. See Paul J. Alexander, "Religious Persecution and Resistance in the Byzantine Empire of the Eighth and Ninth Centuries: Methods and Justifications," *Speculum* 52, no. 2 (1977): 238–64.

70. Luke, 14:23. This line was used for centuries by various Christian churches to justify coercion. It was challenged by Pierre Bayle, a French Protestant who contributed to the Enlightenment, in his influential 1686 book, *A Philosophical Commentary on These Words of the Gospel, Luke 14.23, 'Compel Them to Come In, That My House May Be Full,'* ed. John Kilcullen and Chandran Kukathas (Indianapolis: Liberty Fund Books, 2005). Also see Céline Rohmer, "'Compel Them to Come In!' (Luke 14:23): A Case of Holy Violence?," *Études Théologiques et Religieuses* 94, no. 1 (2019): 109–24.

71. In the United Kingdom, homosexuality was considered a crime until the Sexual Offences Act of 1967, which "permitted homosexual acts between two consenting adults over the age of twenty-one." For an evaluation of the discussions in the United Kingdom at the time, see Patrick Devlin, *The Enforcement of Morals* (Indianapolis: Liberty Fund Books, 2009), p. vi.

72. See Mustafa Akyol, "Lessons of Slavery and Abolition," in *Reopening Muslim Minds,* pp. 61–65.

73. The Qur'anic verse is 90:13. The argument that Islam's original intention to abolish slavery only took place gradually is common in mainstream contemporary Islamic sources.

Chapter 3

74. Leon Louw, "What Is the Rule of Law?" (paper presented at the African Regional Meeting of the Mont Pelerin Society, Nairobi, Kenya, 2007), p. 11. With thanks to Peter Goettler for access to the article.

75. Ernest Gellner, *Postmodernism, Reason and Religion* (London: Routledge, 1992), p. 7.

76. This and all the preceding and following quotes from Evliya Çelebi, with my translation from Turkish, are from Robert Dankoff, Seyit Ali Kahraman, and Yücel Dağlı, *Evliyâ Çelebi Seyahatnâmesi*, Topkapı Sarayı Kütüphanesi Bağdat

304 Numaralı Yazmanın Transkripsiyonu (Istanbul: Yapı Kredi Yayınları, 2006), vol. 1, 128–30.

77. See Ahmet Kuru, *Islam, Authoritarianism, and Underdevelopment: A Global and Historical Comparison* (New York: Cambridge University Press, 2019).

78. Noah Feldman, *The Fall and Rise of the Islamic State* (Princeton, NJ: Princeton University Press, 2008), p. 35.

79. Halide Adıp Adıvar, a towering Turkish female intellectual of the early 20th century, tells the story in *Türkiye'de Şark-Garp ve Amerikan Tesirleri* [East–West and American influences in Turkey] (Istanbul: Can Books, 2009, reprint of 1955 edition), p. 58.

80. Yusuf Küçükdağ, "Zembilli Ali Efendi," *İslâm Ansiklopedisi* (Istanbul: Türkiye Diyanet Vakfı, 2013), vol. 44, 248.

81. The incident and the quotes are from Ishwari Prasad, *History of Medieval India* (Allahabad: Indian Press, 1927), pp. 242–43.

82. Brian Z. Tamanaha, *On the Rule of Law: History, Politics, Theory* (New York: Cambridge University Press, 2004), p. 13. On the same page, Tamanaha also says, "There was no question that the emperor was above the law, for he made the law. Needless to say, this understanding is the very antithesis the rule of law ideal."

83. Guy I. Seidman, "The Origins of Accountability," *Saint Louis University Law Journal* 49, no. 2 (2004/5): 394–95.

84. See Cato Institute, *Unlawful Shield* website, http://www.unlawfulshield.com.

85. Under the Sharia, "immunities against prosecution . . . are totally absent," and "no one can claim any immunity for his or her conduct merely on account of social and official status." John L. Esposito, ed., *The Oxford History of Islam* (New York: Oxford University Press, 1999), p. 149.

86. Three U.S. presidents have been impeached by the U.S. Congress: Andrew Johnson in 1868, Bill Clinton in 1998, and Donald Trump in 2019 and 2021. Richard Nixon resigned in 1974, facing near-certain impeachment. In 2019, Canadian prime minister Justin Trudeau was questioned by the ethics commissioner of the Parliament for an alleged political interference with the justice system. Italian prime minister Silvio Berlusconi faced various corruption

charges while in office by independent prosecutors, such as Antonia Di Pietro. South Korean president Park Geun-hye was impeached in 2017 by the Constitutional Court, and later sentenced to imprisonment, for abuse of power and corruption.

87. "Norwegian PM Fined by Police over Coronavirus Rules Violation," Reuters, April 9, 2021.

88. See the *World Justice Project Rule of Law Index*, https://worldjusticeproject.org/rule-of-law-index/. As of 2019, the countries with the highest rule of law scores were Norway, Finland, and Denmark, whereas no Muslim-majority country made it into the top 25.

89. This comment is from Khayr al-Din al-Tunisi, to whom we will give more attention in the final chapter. The quote is from the translation of his book. Leon Carl Brown, *The Surest Path: The Political Treatise of a Nineteenth-Century Muslim Statesman* (Cambridge, MA: Harvard University Press, 1967), p. 72.

90. Noah Feldman persuasively makes this argument, adding that Ottoman reforms of the 19th century *could have worked* in establishing a liberal order but rather ended in "absolutism." Feldman, *Fall and Rise of the Islamic State*, pp. 59–79.

91. Selim Deringil, "There Is No Compulsion in Religion: On Conversion and Apostasy in the Late Ottoman Empire: 1839–1856," *Comparative Studies in Society and History* 42, no. 3 (2000): 551

92. The edict in question is the Islahat Edict of 1856.

93. Halide Edip Adıvar, "Turkey Faces West," in *Modernist Islam, 1840–1940: A Sourcebook*, ed. Charles Kurzman (New York: Oxford University Press, 2002), p. 215.

94. Articles 8 and 9 of the first Ottoman Constitution, December 23, 1876, http://www.anayasa.gen.tr/1876constitution.htm.

95. In the Ottoman Constitution, the executive was held by the sultan and his Council of Ministers. Legislation was at the hands of a British-style parliament, with two chambers, one of which was freely elected. And the judiciary was left to independent tribunals.

96. For Atatürk's devotion to "unity of powers," see Taha Akyol, *Atatürk'ün İhtilal Hukuku* [Atatürk's law of revolution] (Istanbul: Doğan Kitap, 2012).

97. For a critique of the "unity of powers" under Erdoğan, see "Ergun Özbudun: Kuvvetler ayrılığı gitti kuvvetler birliği geldi" [Separation of powers out, unity of powers in], interview by Taha Akyol, *Karar*, January 25, 2021.

98. See Ruth Austin Miller, "From Fikh to Fascism: The Turkish Republican Adoption of Mussolini's Criminal Code in the Context of Late Ottoman Legal Reform" (PhD diss., Princeton University, 2003). (Miller uses the Turkish term *fıkıh*, which I Anglicized as *fiqh*.)

99. Bernard Lewis, "Islam and Liberal Democracy," *The Atlantic*, February 1993. Lewis also adds that this authoritarian encroachment took place because "social and economic modernization enfeebled or abrogated the religious constraints and intermediate powers that had in various ways limited earlier autocracies."

100. Mohsen Kadivar, "Wilayat al-Faqih and Democracy" in *Islam, the State, and Authority: Medieval Issues and Modern Concerns*, ed. Asma Afsaruddin (New York: Palgrave Macmillan, 2011), p. 214.

101. James I, *The True Law of Free Monarchies and Basilikon Doron*, ed. Daniel Fishclin and Mark Fortier (Toronto: Centre for Reformation and Renaissance Studies, 1996), p. 72.

102. Bernard Lewis, *Faith and Power: Religion and Politics in the Middle East* (New York: Oxford University Press, 2010), p. 160. Lewis—who discovered the letter and has quoted it on various occasions—was also right to note that despotism is a somewhat "modern" problem in the Muslim world.

103. "Montesquieu, Charles de Secondat de," *The Encyclopedia of Libertarianism*, https://www.libertarianism.org/encyclopedia/montesquieu-charles-de-secondat-de.

104. "Montesquieu."

105. J. W. Gough, *John Locke's Political Philosophy: Eight Studies* (Oxford: Oxford University Press, 1964 reprint), pp. 22–23.

106. Khayr al-Din al-Tunisi was wise enough to make this point in his *The Surest Path*: political power must be restrained, "either in the form of a heavenly Shariʿa or a policy based on reason." Kurzman, *Modernist Islam*, p. 45.

107. The accuracy of this famous quote by Abduh is disputed, but it does reflect the spirit of Islamic modernists. See Jonathan A. C. Brown, *Hadith: Muhammad's Legacy in the Medieval and Modern World*, pp. 253–54.

108. This summary of al-Shatibi's approach is from Taha Jabir al-Alwani in *Imam al-Shatibi's Theory of the Higher Objectives and Intents of Islamic Law*, trans. Ahmad al-Raysuni (Herndon, VA: International Institute of Islamic Thought, 2005), p. xi.

109. Muhammad al-Tahir Ibn Ashur, *Treatise on Maqasid al-Sharia*, trans. Mohamed El-Tahir El-Mesawi (Herndon, VA: International Institute of Islamic Thought, 2006), p. 155.

110. For a discussion of this "theological breakthrough," see Mustafa Akyol, "The Theory of *Maqasid* and Its Limits, A Non-Ash'arite Sharia," in *Reopening Muslim Minds*, pp. 79–85.

Chapter 4

111. Alija Izetbegović, *Notes from Prison, 1983–88* (Westport, CT: Praeger, 2002), p. 20.

112. Paul Kelly, *Locke's 'Second Treatise of Government': A Reader's Guide* (London: Bloomsbury, 2007), p. 125. Admittedly, Locke has also been criticized for falling short in his defence of property rights, by defining them in a way that justified colonialization of the Americas. But these critiques seem to disregard the views of Locke "where he affirms that native rights to lands and possessions survive to succeeding generations." See P. Corcoran, "John Locke on Native Right, Colonial Possession, and the Concept of *Vacuum Domicilium*," *European Legacy* 23, no. 3 (2018): 225–50.

113. Shabbir Akhtar, *Islam as Political Religion: The Future of an Imperial Faith* (New York: Routledge, 2010), pp. 217, 219.

114. The quote is from Mohammad Fadel, "No Salvation outside Islam," p. 37.

115. Abdul-Wahab Kayyali, "On the Crisis of Islam: Muslims and the Question of Equality," Al-Jumhuriya.net, November 12, 2020.

116. "I.stanbul'un ikinci fethi de gerçekleşmiştir!" [Istanbul's second conquest has taken place!], *Hakimiyet*, July 14, 2020; "Ayasofya Camii'nin yeniden ibadete açılmasından kâfir ve münafıklardan başkası rahatsız olmaz" [No one except infidels and hypocrites will be disturbed by the reopening of Hagia Sophia], *Milli Gazete*, July 13, 2020. For a critique of this conversion, see Mustafa Akyol, "Would the Prophet Muhammad Convert Hagia Sophia?," *New York Times*, July 20, 2020.

117. "Thoughts on the Hagia Sofia Issue," Yasir Qadhi Facebook page, July 16, 2020, https://www.facebook.com/yasir.qadhi/posts/10158054778088300.

118. Qadhi, "Thoughts on Hagia Sofia."

119. For a relevant article, coauthored by me and my Cato Institute colleague Swaminathan S. Anklesaria Aiyar, see "Why India's Muslims Reach for Liberalism," *New York Times*, October 30, 2020.

120. For this argument on the "contextual" and "interactive" nature of the Qur'an and the Prophetic example, see Mustafa Akyol, "Back to Mecca," in *Reopening Muslim Minds*, pp. 158–78.

121. W. Montgomery Watt, *Muhammad at Medina* (Oxford: Clarendon Press, 1956), p. 221.

122. Watt, *Muhammad at Medina*, p. 221.

123. Watt, *Muhammad at Medina*, p. 221.

124. Article 37, Watt, *Muhammad at Medina*, p. 224.

125. Watt, *Muhammad at Medina*, p. 228.

126. Article 31, Watt, *Muhammad at Medina*, p. 223.

127. According to classical Muslim sources, in the third stage of this story, the Jewish tribe of Banu Qurayza was not merely expelled, all its men were massacred. But the historical truth of this grim story has been challenged by a few modern Muslim historians. Even if it is true, it must be understood in historical context. (See Mustafa Akyol, *Islam without Extremes*, pp. 57–58.) Meanwhile, whether the three major Jewish tribes in Medina, including Banu Qurayza, were in fact signatories of the treaty has been disputed, as their names are not among the Jewish tribes listed in the treaty. One theory is that they were not signatories, but similar agreements might have been signed with them. See

Uri Rubin, "The 'Constitution of Medina': Some Notes," *Studia Islamica* 62 (1985): 9–10.

128. The document known as the "Pact of Umar" reads as a letter written to Umar Ibn al-Khattab (caliph from 634 to 644) by the Christians of Syria and Palestine after the conquest of those territories in 637. But many historians, both Muslim and non-Muslim, think the text is actually from much later, the time of the Umayyad ruler Umar bin 'Abd al-'Aziz (caliph from 717 to 720), as it reflects the existing attitudes toward minorities in the Byzantine and Sassanid Empires. See Oded Peri, *Christianity under Islam in Jerusalem: The Question of the Holy Sites in Early Ottoman Times* (Leiden: Brill, 2001), p. 52. Also see Mustafa Fayda, "Eş-Şürûtü'l Ömeriyye," *İslâm Ansiklopedisi* 39 (2010): 273–74. Meanwhile it is worth noting that many Muslim rulers, out of pragmatism, "overlooked [the] flagrant violations of the stipulations of the Pact of 'Umar." Cohen, *Under the Crescent and Cross*, p. 196.

129. Watt, *Muhammad at Medina*, p. 225.

130. Asma Afsaruddin, "Tolerance and Pluralism in Islamic Thought and Praxis," in *Toleration in Comparative Perspective*, ed. Vicki A. Spencer (Lanham, MD: Lexington Books, 2017), p. 110.

Chapter 5

131. *Sahih al-Muslim*, 1847.

132. Qur'an 4:59 (italics added).

133. Article 9 of the Saudi Basic Law refers to "the Islamic Creed, which demands allegiance and obedience to God, to His Prophet and to *the rulers*," https://www.saudiembassy.net/basic-law-governance (italics added).

134. "Former Mufti: Obeying Sisi Is Obedience to Prophet," *Al-Masry Al-Youm*, August 4, 2015, https://egyptindependent.com/former-mufti-obeying-sisi-obedience-prophet/.

135. Leila Chamankhah, *The Conceptualization of Guardianship in Iranian Intellectual History (1800–1989)* (Cham, Switzerland: Palgrave Macmillan, 2019), p. 219.

136. Asma Afsaruddin, "The Qur'an as a Political Programme," *Oasis* 13, no. 25 (2017): 14–21.

137. Richard P. Mitchell, *The Society of the Muslim Brothers* (New York: Oxford University Press, 1993), p. 300.

138. Mustafa Öztürk, "İslam Tefsir Geleneğinde Yorum Manipülasyonu: Ulu'l-Emr' Kavramı Örneği" [Manipulative interpretation in Islamic tradition: the example of *ulu'l amr*], *İslamiyat* 3 (2000): 82.

139. For this argument, see Kuru, *Islam, Authoritarianism, and Underdevelopment*, pp. 42–45.

140. For these various views on the definition of *ulu'l amr,* see Talip Türcan, "Ülü'l-Emr," *İslam Ansiklopedisi*, 42 (2012): 295–97.

141. George Makdisi, *Ibn 'Aqil: Religion and Culture in Classical Islam* (Edinburgh: Edinburgh University Press, 1997), p. 167. In the rest of his paragraph, translated by Makdisi, Ibn 'Aqil also says the following: "This type of [unfree] individual is never able to care for himself, but is always under someone else's care. He is, like a grazing sheep, in need of a shepherd. What good has he derived from reason? What influence has the revealed law had on his education? God preserve us from forsaking His tutorship and guidance, and contenting ourselves with the restraint of His creatures, our peers!"

142. Namık Kemal, "Wa shawirhum fi'l-amr" [And seek their counsel in the matter], *Hürriyet*, London, July 20, 1868, pp. 1–2. Translation from Turkish and introduction by M. Şükrü Hanioğlu in Kurzman, *Modernist Islam*, p. 144.

143. Kurzman, *Modernist Islam*, p. 144.

144. One such hadith is the one quoted in the epigraph of this chapter: "You should hear and obey the ruler, even if he flogs your back and takes your wealth." *Sahih al-Muslim*, 1847. For others and how they are used for justifying authoritarianism, see Mustafa Akyol, "The Divine Rights of Muslim Kings," in *Reopening Muslim Minds*, pp. 150–52.

145. Asma Afsaruddin, *Contemporary Issues in Islam* (Edinburgh: Edinburgh University Press, 2015), p. 29.

146. Fakhr al-Din al-Razi also refers to this incident in his Great Commentary while interpreting 4:59. *Tefsir-i Kebir* (Ankara: Huzur Yayınevi, 1991), vol. 8, p. 106.

147. This interpretation of 4:59 is uncommon but not unprecedented. According to both companion Ibn Abbas and the early exegete al-Suddi (d. 744), the phrase *ulu'l amr* referred to "various military commanders during the lifetime of the Prophet." Afsaruddin, *Contemporary Issues in Islam*, p. 30. Fakhr al-Din al-Razi also notes two views that limited *ulu'l amr* to specific people: "commanders of *sariyya*," or "rightly guided caliphs," that is, the first four caliphs recognized by the Sunni tradition. *Tefsir-i Kebir*, vol. 8, p. 106.

Chapter 6

148. Hashemi, *Islam, Secularism and Liberal Democracy*, p. 94.

149. That means I moved away from the views that imply supernatural interventions by God in the natural universe—such as in the theory of intelligent design—to the view that God created the natural universe and set up the laws by which it naturally operates. Consequently, I no longer had a problem with the Darwinian theory of evolution, but with its atheistic interpretations by Richard Dawkins and the like. That is because I realized theistic naturalism not only allows better science but also offers better theology.

150. See Mustafa Akyol, *The Islamic Jesus* (New York: St. Martin's Press, 2017), pp. 158–61.

151. Dimitri Gutas, *Greek Thought, Arabic Culture: The Graeco-Arabic Translation Movement in Baghdad and Early Abbasid Society* (New York: Routledge, 1998), p. 192.

152. See Akyol, *Reopening Muslim Minds*, pp. 1–10, 109–30.

153. Sidney H. Griffith, "The Monk in the Emir's Majlis," in *The Majlis: Interreligious Encounters in Medieval Islam*, ed. Hava Lazarus Yafeh (Wiesbaden: Otto Harrassowitz, 1999), p. 40.

154. Zachary Karabell, *Peace Be upon You: Fourteen Centuries of Muslim, Christian, and Jewish Conflict and Cooperation* (New York: Vintage Books, 2008), p. 49.

155. Griffith, "Monk in the Emir's Majlis," p. 42.

156. Griffith, "Monk in the Emir's Majlis," p. 42.

157. Qur'an, 29:46.

158. Sidney H. Griffith, *The Church in the Shadow of the Mosque: Christians and Muslims in the World of Islam* (Princeton, NJ: Princeton University Press, 2008), p. 103.

159. See *1001 Inventions* website, https://1001inventions.com.

160. See Mustafa Akyol, "Freedom in the Muslim World," Cato Institute Economic Development Bulletin no. 33, August 25, 2020.

161. Qur'an, 2:111, 21:24, 27:64.

162. The most referred "verse of the sword" was 9:5, which read, "Wherever you encounter the idolaters, kill them." Many medieval Muslim jurists took this as an "abrogation" of the earlier verses that command peace, tolerance, or patience, but alternative views have been revived in the modern era. See Akyol, "The Abrogation of Mecca," in *Reopening Muslim Minds*, pp. 176–78.

163. The verse about Moses speaking to the Pharaoh is 20:44. Al-Razi's comments are from his exegesis on 3:186 in this *Tefsir-i Kebir* (Grand Commentary).

164. Al-Razi, *Tefsir-i Kebir.*

165. Mustafa Akyol, "Muslims Should Disarm Islamophobia with Kindness," *New York Times*, February 27, 2020.

166. "Ban the Koran in the Netherlands, says far-right leader Wilders," Euronews, March 5, 2017.

167. The true freedom of speech advocates referred to here include Danish journalist and Cato Institute senior fellow Flemming Rose, who, in a public debate in 2015 challenged Wilder's authoritarian ambitions against Islam and Muslims. I wrote about this debate in "Is Free Speech Good for Muslims?," *New York Times*, March 27, 2017.

168. Jonathan Brown Facebook page, March 15, 2020, https://www.facebook.com/jonathanacbrown/posts/10158111583684850.

Chapter 7

169. Muhammad Akram Khan, *What Is Wrong with Islamic Economics? Analysing the Present State and Future Agenda* (Cheltenham, UK: Edward Elgar, 2013), p. xv.

170. Ovamir Anjum, *Politics Law and Community in Islamic Thought* (New York: Cambridge University Press, 2012), p. 267.

171. The textual origin of this popular hadith is hard to map. In Ottoman sources, it is found in the Forty Hadith collection by Âlî Mustafa Efendi. Hasan Aksoy, *Mustafa Âlî'nin Manzum Kırk Hadis Tercümeleri* (Istanbul: Marmara University, 1991), pp. 52–53. Its engraving at Istanbul's Grand Bazaar is on the Fesçiler (Fez Makers) Gate, and it was handwritten by calligrapher Hattat Sami during the reconstruction of the complex in the 1890s at the time of Sultan Abdulhamid II.

172. *Jami al-Tirmidhi*, Book 14, Hadith 7.

173. Casim Avcı, "Kureyş," *İslam Ansiklopedisi*, vol. 26, p. 442.

174. Andrew Rippin, "Trade and Commerce," *Encyclopedia of the Qur'an* (Leiden: Brill, 2001), vol. 5, p. 311.

175. Qur'an, 2:16, 5:12, 7:8–9, 9:111, 27:5.

176. Charles C. Torrey, "The Commercial-Theological Terms in the Koran" (PhD diss., University of Strasburg, 1892).

177. Qur'an, 25:7, 25:20.

178. Qur'an, 4:29 (italics added).

179. Qur'an, 2:282.

180. For a short evaluation of the sources on Islam and capitalism, see Abbas Mirakhor and Hossein Askari, *Ideal Islamic Economy: An Introduction* (New York: Palgrave Macmillan, 2017), pp. 71–73.

181. Al-Samhudi, *Wafa al-Wafa* (Cairo, 1326 AH), vol. 1, p. 540; quoted in M. J. Kister, "The Market of the Prophet," *Journal of the Economic and Social History of the Orient* 8 (1965): 274.

182. Kister, "Market of the Prophet," pp. 275–76.

183. *Bulugh al-Maram*, Book 7, "Business Transactions," hadith 38. A shorter version of the same narration is also found in *Sunan Abi Dawud*, Book 24, "Book of Wages," hadith 35 (italics added).

184. Benedikt Koehler, *Early Islam and the Birth of Capitalism* (Lanham, MD: Lexington Books, 2014), pp. 11–12.

185. Gene W. Heck, *Charlemagne, Muhammad, and the Arab Roots of Capitalism* (Berlin: Walter de Gruyter GmbH, 2006), p. 3.

186. Heck, *Arab Roots of Capitalism*, p. 81.

187. Timur Kuran, *The Long Divergence: How Islamic Law Held Back the Middle East* (Princeton, NJ: Princeton University Press, 2011), pp. 49–50.

188. Kuran, *The Long Divergence*, p. 50.

189. Robert W. Hillman, "Limited Liability in Historical Perspective," *Washington and Lee Law Review* 54 (1997): 620.

190. Heck, *Arab Roots of Capitalism*, p. 3.

191. Heck, *Arab Roots of Capitalism*, pp. 161–258; Koehler, *Early Islam*, pp. 187–212.

192. Dániel Oláh, "The Amazing Arab Scholar Who Beat Adam Smith by Half a Millennium," *Evonomics*, June 17, 2017.

193. Ibn Khaldun, *The Muqaddimah: An Introduction to History,* trans. Franz Rosenthal (Princeton, NJ: Princeton University Press, 1967), vol. 2, pp. 103–4.

194. "Reagan Cites Islamic Scholar," *New York Times*, October 2, 1981; Ronald Reagan, "There They Go Again," *New York Times,* February 18, 1993.

195. Murat Çızakça, *Islamic Capitalism and Finance: Origins, Evolution and the Future* (Cheltenham, UK: Edward Elgar, 2011), p. xv.

196. There is a large literature on the mass murders, enslaved labor, political purges, and other forms of brutal oppression under communist dictatorships, such as the former Soviet Union, People's Republic of China, and Cambodia under the Khmer Rouge. Even in Yugoslavia, probably the mildest of all communist regimes of the 20th century, the promise of equality was betrayed by what Milovan Đjilas called "the new class"—which consisted of communist party members—that "uses, enjoys and disposes of nationalized property." See *The New Class: An Analysis of the Communist System* (New York: Harvest/HBJ Book, 1982).

197. Qur'an, 2:177

198. Timur Kuran, "Zakat: Islam's Missed Opportunity to Limit Predatory Taxation," *Public Choice* 182 (2020): 395.

199. The oft-quoted verse is 59:7, which reads, "Whatever gains God has turned over to His Messenger from the inhabitants of the villages belong to God, the Messenger, kinsfolk, orphans, the needy, the traveller in need—this is so that *they do not just circulate among those of you who are rich*" (italics added). Islamic socialists

have repeatedly used the verse to justify redistribution of private wealth, but the verse only referred to spoils of war, which is a quite different category than wealth acquired by personal work or inheritance.

200. See Akyol, "Freedom in the Muslim World," p. 2.

201. Alija Izetbegović, *Islam between East and West* (Oak Brook, IL: American Trust Publications, 1984), p. xxix.

202. Izetbegović, *Islam between East and West*, p. 207.

203. Izetbegović, *Islam between East and West*, p. 208.

204. Siraj Sait and Hilary Lim, *Land, Law, and Islam: Property and Human Rights in the Muslim World* (London: Zed Books, 2006), p. 150.

205. Kuru, *Islam, Authoritarianism, and Underdevelopment*, p. 7.

206. See Timur Kuran, "The Absence of the Corporation in Islamic Law: Origins and Persistence," *American Journal of Comparative Law* 53, no. 4 (2005): 785–834. Also see Kuran, *The Long Divergence*.

207. Bernard Lewis, "Islam and Liberal Democracy," *The Atlantic*, February 1993.

208. "Khuṭbat Ismāʿīl Bey Gaṣbrinkī," trans. ʿAbd al-Wahhāb al-Najjār, *al-Manār*, vol. 10 (1907), p. 670; quoted in Leor Halevi, *Modern Things on Trial: Islam's Global and Material Reformation in the Age of Rida, 1865–1935* (New York: Columbia University Press, 2019), p. 116.

209. Kuran, *Long Divergence*, p. 97.

210. See Zafer Toprak, "From Liberalism to Solidarism: The Ottoman Economic Mind in the Age of the Nation State (1820–1920)," in *Studies in Ottoman Social and Economic Life*, ed. Raoul Motika, Christoph Herzog, and Michael Ursinus (Heidelberg: Heidelberger Orientverlag, 1999), pp. 171–90. Toprak notes that the "libertarian economic milieu of Tanzimat regime" was later replaced by nationalist and statist policies.

211. Quote from Şevket Pamuk, *Uneven Centuries: Economic Development of Turkey since 1820* (Princeton, NJ: Princeton University Press, 2018), p. 140. Pamuk, a prominent Turkish economic historian, also calculates that from 1820 to 1923—the period largely marked by Tanzimat liberalism—the gross domestic product per capita in today's Turkey, adjusted to 1990 U.S. dollars, rose from $720

to $1,150. That amounts to an annual growth of 0.5 percent, while the same figure for Western Europe was 1.2 percent. "Turkey did better than the developing countries as a whole, as well as Asia and Africa," he adds (pp. 135–36).

212. "At the end of the eighteenth century, some 20,000 *waqfs* existed in the Ottoman Empire with a total annual revenue of one-third of annual government revenues and one-half to two-thirds of its arable land." Umar F. Moghul, *A Socially Responsible Islamic Finance: Character and the Common Good* (New York: Palgrave Macmillan, 2017), p. 217.

213. As I demonstrated in "Freedom in the Muslim World," most Arab republics still have very low levels of economic freedom, compared with Arab monarchies, many of which are more "conducive to the rule of law and less corruption; exhibit more secure property rights; have bigger financial systems; and experience faster economic growth."

214. Qur'an, 2:274–75, 2:279, 3:130, 30:39. It is said in the tradition that the verses that ban *riba* were among the last ones to be revealed, so the Prophet did not have much time to clarify them. For a discussion on the meaning of *riba*, see Seyyed Hossein Nasr, ed., *The Study Qur'an* (New York: HarperCollins, 2015), pp. 120–21.

215. Masudul Alam Choudhury, "Usury," *Encyclopedia of the Qur'an*, vol. 5, p. 407.

216. The term "pre-modern banking system" is from Murat Çızakça, "Economic Dimensions of Foundations in the Ottoman Era," in *Philanthropy in Turkey: Citizens, Foundations and the Pursuit of Social Justice* (Istanbul: Tüsev Publications, 2006), p. 33. The figure 19 percent is from one of the most detailed studies on Ottoman cash foundations: Timur Kuran and Jared Rubin, "The Financial Power of the Powerless: Interest Rates and Socio-Economic Status under Partial Rule of Law," *Economic Journal* 128 (2018): 762.

217. Ali Allawi, foreword to *Ideal Islamic Economy: An Introduction* by Abbas Mirhakor and Hossein Askari (New York: Palgrave Macmillan, 2017), p. xiii.

218. The quote is from Fazlur Rahman, who inferred this meaning of *riba* according to his analysis of the relevant Islamic texts to conclude that "*Riba* is an exorbitant increment whereby the capital sum is doubled several-fold, against a fixed extension of the term of payment of the debt." Fazlur Rahman, "Riba and Interest," *Islamic Studies* 3, no. 1 (1964): 6, 40.

219. Allawi, foreword to *Ideal Islamic Economy*, p. xiii.

220. Michael O'Sullivan, "Interest, Usury, and the Transition from 'Muslim' to 'Islamic' Banks, 1908–1958," *International Journal of Middle East Studies* 52 (2020): 261.

221. O'Sullivan, "Interest, Usury," p. 263.

222. Timur Kuran, "Banks and Banking, Modern," *Encyclopedia of Islam*, 3rd ed. (Leiden: Brill, 2015), p. 66.

223. Kuran, "Banks and Banking."

224. Kuran, "Banks and Banking."

225. Ariana Mirza, "Fraud, in the Name of God," *Qantara.de*, December 1, 2006.

226. "Turkey's Erdogan Calls Interest Rates 'Mother of All Evil'; Lira Slides," Reuters, May 11, 2018.

227. See Ragip Soylu, "Turkey's Lira: The Story of an Epic Downfall," *Middle East Eye*, November 24, 2020; and "Turkey's Long, Painful Economic Crisis Grinds On," *New York Times*, July 8, 2019.

228. "İslam iktisadı krizden çıkışın anahtarıdır" [Islamic economics is the key to the exit out of the crisis], TRT Haber, June 14, 2020. Steve Hanke, prominent economist and a senior fellow at the Cato Institute, observed the following: "Erdogan believes that low-interest rates cause low inflation and that high-interest rates cause high inflation. This general notion comes out of Islamic finance and is obviously totally incorrect. Because interest rates follow the course of inflation, not the other way around." (Personal correspondence with Hanke on January 21, 2020).

229. "Türkiye'den 5 inşaat firması dünyada en fazla ihale alan ilk 10 firma arasında" [5 construction companies in Turkey are among the global top 10], Euronews, July 12, 2020. The data are originally from World Bank, "Featured Rankings, 1990 to 2019," https://ppi.worldbank.org/en/snapshots/rankings.

230. For a discussion of the values of "ethical bourgeoisie," see Deirdre N. McCloskey, *The Bourgeois Virtues: Ethics for an Age of Commerce* (Chicago: University of Chicago Press, 2010).

231. Allawi, foreword to *Ideal Islamic Economy*, p. xii.

232. For this definition of economic freedom, see Vásquez and McMahon, *Human Freedom Index*, 2020, p. 12.

233. The economic freedom scores of Muslim-majority countries are in fact relatively better than their personal freedom scores, but they are still low compared with world averages, the lowest of them being in Arab republics with socialist foundations: Libya, Algeria, Sudan, and Egypt. See Akyol, "Freedom in the Muslim World," pp. 9–10.

Chapter 8

234. Danny Postel, "Liberalism, Internationalism and Iran Today," in *Liberalism for a New Century*, ed. Neil Jumonville and Kevin Mattson (Los Angeles: University of California Press, 2007), p. 200.

235. For Enlightenment thinkers such as Denis Diderot, Immanuel Kant, and Johann Gottfried Herder who raised objections to European colonialism, see Sankar Muthu, *Enlightenment against Empire* (Princeton, NJ: Princeton University Press, 2003).

236. Albert Hourani, *Arabic Thought in the Liberal Age, 1798–1939* (Cambridge: Cambridge University Press, 1983), p. 50.

237. Danny Postel quotes that view "from a friend of mine" while also referring to similarly anti-liberal views by various leftist intellectuals, such as Immanuel Wallerstein, Samir Amin, and Slavoj Zizek, in "Liberalism, Internationalism and Iran Today," pp. 198, 235.

238. Jabarti's critique of French colonial rule with liberal arguments—originally in his *Tarikh Muddat al-Faransis bi-Misr*—are quoted here in Stephen Andrew Bush, "Continuity and Change in the Concept of Freedom through Three Generations of the Modern Arab Renaissance" (master's thesis, University of Texas at Austin, 2011), pp. 14–15.

239. Bush, "Continuity and Change," pp. 14–15.

240. Bush, "Continuity and Change," pp. 14–15.

241. Bush, "Continuity and Change," p. 16.

242. Daniel L. Newman, *An Imam in Paris: Account of a Stay in France by an Egyptian Cleric, 1826–1831* (London: Saqi Books, 2004), p. 205.

243. Bush, "Continuity and Change," pp. 30–31.

244. The word *serbesti* existed in Ottoman terminology, referring to a special kind of *timar* (land grant) without taxes paid to the central government. In light of the French Revolution, however, Morali el-Sayyid Ali Efendi, the Ottoman ambassador in Paris, used the term in his report translated as *liberté*. Bernard Lewis, *Islam in History: Ideas, People, and Events in the Middle East* (Chicago: Open Court Publishing, 2001), pp. 323–24.

245. The term "Islamic liberalism" was highlighted by Leonard Binder in *Islamic Liberalism: A Critique of Development Ideologies* (Chicago: University of Chicago Press, 1988). For a more encompassing survey of the Muslim thinkers who can be defined as pioneers of Islamic liberalism, see Charles Kurzman, ed., *Liberal Islam: A Sourcebook* (New York: Oxford University Press, 1998).

246. Şerif Mardin, *The Genesis of Young Ottoman Thought: A Study in the Modernization of Turkish Political Ideas* (New York: Syracuse University, 2000), p. 4. The term Mardin translated as "Young Ottomans," *Yeni Osmanlılar*, can also be translated as "New Ottomans," which I prefer.

247. Kurzman, *Modernist Islam*, p. 6.

248. The comment is from Ahmet Kabaklı, a Turkish political conservative, who shared this observation only in a critical tone. Ahmet Kabaklı, *Şiir İncelemeleri* (1992, p. 176), quoted in Adem Çalışkan, "Namık Kemal's Ode to Freedom and Its Analysis," *Journal of International Social Research* 7, no. 31 (2014): 87–88.

249. Namık Kemal, "Wa shawirhum fi'l amr" (And seek their counsel in the matter), *Hürriyet*, July 20, 1868, pp. 1–2, translation and introduction by M. Şükrü Hanioğlu, in Kurzman, *Modernist Islam*, pp. 144–45.

250. Mardin, *Genesis of Young Ottoman Thought*, pp. 308–9.

251. Alp Eren Topal, *Sürgünde Muhalefet: Namık Kemal'in Hürriyet Gazetesi, 1868–1869* (Istanbul: VakıfBank Kültür Yayınları, 2019) pp. 2, 15–16 (from Turkish with my translation).

252. The arguments on "consultation" (*shura*) and "disagreement" (*ihtilaf*) were advanced in *Hürriyet*, "Mülahaza: İhtilafu Ümmeti Rahmetun," vol. 2, and "Usul-i Meşveret," vols. 12, 13, 16, 18. The quote on "the spark of truth" reads, "Bârika-i hakikat, müsâdeme-i efkârdan doğar."

253. For Kemal's words on Montesquieu, see Mardin, *Genesis of Young Ottoman Thought*, p. 333.

254. Namık Kemal, *Renan Müdafaanâmesi*, ed. M. Fuad Köprülü (Ankara: Milli Kültür Yayinlari, 1962), p. 19. The book was written by Kemal in 1883 on Midilli, also known as Lesbos, an Aegean island where he was exiled after the abrupt end of the constitutional regime that he had spearheaded.

255. Scholar Alp Eren Topal shares these observations in the introduction of this two-volume translation of *Hürriyet*, a significant contribution to the literature on New Ottomans and Islamic modernization. Topal, *Sürgünde Muhalefet: Namık Kemal'in Hürriyet Gazetesi, 1868–1869* (Istanbul: VakıfBank Kültür Yayınları, 2019), vol. 1, p. 34.

256. Leon Carl Brown, *The Surest Path: The Political Treatise of a Nineteenth-Century Muslim Statesman* (Cambridge, MA: Center for Middle Eastern Studies, Harvard University, 1967), p. 72.

257. Leon Carl Brown, *The Surest Path*, pp. 47, 54.

258. Leon Carl Brown, *The Surest Path*, p. 79.

259. Leon Carl Brown, *The Surest Path*, pp. 160–62.

260. Cemil Meriç, *Mağaradakiler* [Those in the cave] (İstanbul: İletişim Yayınları, 1998), p. 171.

261. Meriç, *Mağaradakiler*, p. 171.

262. Leon Carl Brown, *The Surest Path*, pp. 52–53.

263. Leon Carl Brown, *The Surest Path*, pp. 52, 72.

264. Leon Carl Brown, *The Surest Path*, p. 45.

265. Hourani, *Arabic Thought in the Liberal Age*.

266. Klaus Wivel, *The Last Supper: The Plight of Christians in Arab Lands* (New York: New Vessel Press, 2016), p. 69.

267. Kurzman, *Modernist Islam*, p. 255.

268. Taha Akyol, "Cedidcilik," in *İslam Ansiklopedisi* (İstanbul: Türkiye Diyanet Vakfı, 1993), vol. 7, pp. 212–13.

269. In the words of scholar Mansoor Moaddel, "Islamic fundamentalism has primarily been a reaction to the secular change promoted and supported by the

modern national state, which was first formed in Egypt, Iran, and Turkey in the early 1920s and later in other Middle Eastern and North African countries. In countries where the state turned overly secularist, exclusivist, authoritarian, and interventionist, the fundamentalist movement also turned extremist and exclusivist." Moaddel, *The Clash of Values: Islamic Fundamentalism versus Liberal Nationalism* (New York: Columbia University Press 2020), p. 31.

270. Shabbir Akhtar, *Islam as Political Religion: The Future of an Imperial Faith* (New York: Routledge, 2010), p. 219.

271. Lewis, *Islam in History*, p. 336.

272. See Esther Webman, *The Global Impact of the Protocols of the Elders of Zion: A Century-Old Myth* (Taylor & Francis, 2012), pp. 175–227.

273. Cohen, *Under the Crescent and Cross*, pp. 282–83.

274. Christopher de Bellaigue, *The Islamic Enlightenment: The Struggle between Faith and Reason, 1798 to Modern Times* (New York: Liveright Publishing, 2017), p. 104.

275. The quotes in the paragraph are from Elizabeth Thompson's book *How the West Stole Democracy from the Arabs: The Syrian Arab Congress of 1920 and the Destruction of Its Historic Liberal-Islamic Alliance* (New York: Atlantic Monthly Press, 2020), p. 1.

276. Postel, "Liberalism, Internationalism and Iran Today," p. 195.

277. Postel, "Liberalism, Internationalism and Iran Today," p. 199.

278. Reza Afshari, *Human Rights in Iran: The Abuse of Cultural Relativism* (Philadelphia: University of Pennsylvania Press, 2011), pp. 5, 199; Adam Tarock, "The Muzzling of the Liberal Press in Iran," *Third World Quarterly* 22, no. 4 (2001): 585–602.

279. "Citing Nur Fitri Case, Najib Says Liberalism a Threat to Muslim Identity," *Malay Mail*, May 14, 2015.

280. "Malaysian PM Warns against Liberalism, Pluralism," Asia One, July 19, 2012 (italics added).

281. "Jewels, Handbags, Cash: What Former Malaysian PM Najib Razak Allegedly Stole," *Sydney Morning Herald*, July 4, 2018.

282. Mustafa Akyol, "Egypt's Fascist 'Liberals,'" *Hürriyet Daily News*, September 7, 2013.

283. S. Akbar Zaidi, "Liberals Are Dangerous," *The Dawn*, December 12, 2017.

Epilogue

284. Quote from Dr. Khaled Abou El Fadl's sermon at the Usuli Institute, September 25, 2020, "Death by Doctrine of the 'Legitimacy of the Usurpers,'" https://soundcloud.com/usuli/usuli-institute-khutbah-death-by-doctrine-of-the-legitimacy-of-the-usurpers-25-sept-2020.

285. With thanks to Rasheed Dar, who coined the term *la-ikrahiyya* in a personal conversation in New York City in the fall of 2018.

286. Hourani, *Arabic Thought in the Liberal Age*, p. 88.

About the Author

Mustafa Akyol is a senior fellow at the Cato Institute's Center for Global Liberty and Prosperity, where he focuses on the intersection of public policy, Islam, and modernity. Since 2013, he has also been a contributing opinion writer for the *New York Times*, covering politics and religion in the Muslim world. Before joining the Cato Institute in 2018, Akyol worked for more than a decade as an opinion columnist for two Turkish newspapers, *Hurriyet Daily News* and *Star*—until they were co-opted and transformed into pro-government propaganda outlets. His articles have also appeared in a wide range of other publications, including the *Wall Street Journal*, the *Washington Post*, *The Atlantic*, *Foreign Affairs*, *Foreign Policy*, *Newsweek*, *Al-Monitor*, *First Things*, *The Forward*, the *Weekly Standard*, the *Financial Times*, the *London Times*,

The Guardian, the *Washington Times*, and Pakistan's *The Dawn*. He has appeared frequently on CNN, BBC, NPR, and Al-Jazeera English and on prominent TV shows such as *Fareed Zakaria GPS* and *HARDtalk*. His TED talk on "Faith versus Tradition in Islam" has been watched by more than 1.2 million viewers.

He is the author of *Reopening Muslim Minds: A Return to Reason, Freedom, and Tolerance* (2021), *The Islamic Jesus: How the King of the Jews Became a Prophet of the Muslims* (2017), and *Islam without Extremes: A Muslim Case for Liberty* (2011).

Libertarianism.org

Liberty. It's a simple idea and the linchpin of a complex system of values and practices: justice, prosperity, responsibility, toleration, cooperation, and peace. Many people believe that liberty is the core political value of modern civilization itself, the one that gives substance and form to all the other values of social life. They're called libertarians.

Libertarianism.org is the Cato Institute's treasury of resources about the theory and history of liberty. The book you're holding is a small part of what Libertarianism.org has to offer. In addition to hosting classic texts by historical libertarian figures and original articles from modern-day thinkers, Libertarianism.org publishes podcasts, videos, online introductory courses, and books on a variety of topics within the libertarian tradition.

Cato Institute

Founded in 1977, the Cato Institute is a public policy research foundation dedicated to broadening the parameters of policy debate to allow consideration of more options that are consistent with the principles of limited government, individual liberty, and peace. To that end, the Institute strives to achieve greater involvement of the intelligent, concerned lay public in questions of policy and the proper role of government.

The Institute is named for *Cato's Letters*, libertarian pamphlets that were widely read in the American Colonies in the early 18th century and played a major role in laying the philosophical foundation for the American Revolution.

Despite the achievement of the nation's Founders, today, virtually no aspect of life is free from government encroachment. A pervasive intolerance for individual rights is shown by government's arbitrary intrusions into private economic transactions and its disregard for civil liberties. And while freedom around the globe has notably increased in the past several decades, many countries have moved in the opposite direction, and most governments still do not respect or safeguard the wide range of civil and economic liberties.

To address those issues, the Cato Institute undertakes an extensive publications program on the complete spectrum of policy issues. Books, monographs, and shorter studies are commissioned to examine the federal budget, Social Security, regulation, military spending, international trade, and myriad other issues. Major policy conferences are held throughout the year, from which papers are published thrice yearly in the *Cato Journal*. The Institute also publishes the quarterly magazine *Regulation*.

In order to maintain its independence, the Cato Institute accepts no government funding. Contributions are received from foundations, corporations, and individuals, and other revenue is generated from the sale of publications. The Institute is a nonprofit, tax-exempt, educational foundation under Section 501(c)3 of the Internal Revenue Code.

CATO INSTITUTE
1000 Massachusetts Avenue NW
Washington, DC 20001
www.cato.org